Whispers of the Gods

Whispers of the Gods

Tales from Baseball's Golden Age, Told by the Men Who Played It

Peter Golenbock

ROWMAN & LITTLEFIELD
Lanham • Boulder • New York • London

Published by Rowman & Littlefield
An imprint of The Rowman & Littlefield Publishing Group, Inc.
4501 Forbes Boulevard, Suite 200, Lanham, Maryland 20706
www.rowman.com

86-90 Paul St, London, EC2A 4NE, United Kingdom

Distributed by NATIONAL BOOK NETWORK

British Library Cataloguing in Publication Information Available

Library of Congress Cataloging-in-Publication Data

Names: Golenbock, Peter, 1946– author.
Title: Whispers of the gods : tales from baseball's golden age, told by the
    men who played it / by Peter Golenbock.
Description: Lanham, Maryland : Rowman & Littlefield Publishing Group,
    [2021] | Summary: "Bestselling author Peter Golenbock brings to life
    baseball greats from the 1940s, '50s, and '60s with Whispers of the
    Gods. Like the enduring classic The Glory of Their Times, this book is
    based on hundreds of hours of taped interviews featuring the likes of
    Roy Campanella, Ted Williams, Phil Rizzuto, Jim Bouton, Stan Musial, and
    more"—Provided by publisher.
Identifiers: LCCN 2021014374 (print) | LCCN 2021014375 (ebook) | ISBN
    9781538154878 (cloth) | ISBN 9781538154885 (epub)
Subjects: LCSH: Baseball players—United States—Biography. |
    Baseball—United States—History—Biography.
Classification: LCC GV863.A1 G65 2021 (print) | LCC GV863.A1 (ebook) |
    DDC 796.357092/273 [B]—dc23
LC record available at https://lccn.loc.gov/2021014374
LC ebook record available at https://lccn.loc.gov/2021014375

Contents

Foreword

$\mathcal{W}$hen Henry Aaron died in January 2021, just short of his eighty-seventh birthday, he became the tenth member of the Baseball Hall of Fame to pass in a distressing nine months. Ruefully, Keith Olbermann noted that "All of the baseball cards are dying." I knew exactly what he meant.

It was the cards of 1950s stars like Aaron that forever linked my generation with its baseball idols. Even today, on the dark slope of life, I cannot hold a 1950s Topps card without feeling, in a sensual way, the heat of a Bronx sidewalk, the thrill of fanning the cards to see "who I got," the taste of a Mission orange soda, the smell and peculiar feel of the pink slab of bubblegum, and the thrill of flipping my hard-earned prizes toward the wall of our apartment house, hoping to vanquish my mates. I was young only yesterday.

Like Peter Golenbock, I have spent a lifetime thinking and writing about the great American game. Unlike him, however, I have had few friends who were former players. I luxuriated in the game's recorded history, forming friendships with folks I had never met, especially those who died before I was born. Yet like Peter I was a child of the 1950s and 1960s, when I came to love the game and create my personal pantheon.

In the 1950s, we were measuring ourselves amid an age of heroes—those who had won the War and rid the world of fascism. As we entered young adulthood in the 1960s, we were entering into another age of heroes, the maelstrom of the civil rights struggle, winning battles if not, as we see all too clearly now, the war. By the 1970s we "put away childish things" and gravitated to antiheroes. In baseball it was out with Babe Ruth and Lou Gehrig and in with Jim Bouton and Sparky Lyle. Peter was close with Bouton then, as I was to be later on, and with Lyle in *The Bronx Zoo* he created an all-time sports bestseller.

As it has turned out, the heroes of our youth did not disappear as we aged; they hibernated. Baseball may not matter now as it did then, but magically *they* do. We no longer need them as models of rectitude, talismans against evil—what would Jackie do in this fix, one might wonder . . . or the Duke? As we hit middle age and beyond, and look at our lives in the rearview mirror, the ballplayers reemerge in all their old vigor.

Time mercifully casts a hazy aura over our ancient missteps; our baseball heroes, more burnished than tarnished for reemerging as real people, become welcoming guides to the lost world of our youth. How good it is to have as companions on that journey Ted Williams or Stan Musial, Roy Campanella or Monte Irvin, still in their baseball-card poses but now in three dimensions. Thank you, Peter!

To the anticipated cavil that *Whispers of the Gods* is just the latest in a long line of baseball books for boomers, I draw your attention to the subtitle: *Tales from Baseball's Golden Age Told by the Men Who Played It*. The Golden Age of Baseball (or movies or rock and roll or most anything else) is not this decade or that one, but the year in which you hit puberty and everything changed. It cannot be long before middle-aged baseball writers create paeans to the game of the 1980s.

Baseball is a backward-looking institution. It pleases us to think that giants once strode the earth and their like will not be seen again. This is baloney of course. But serve it up between two slices of bread, with a shmeer of nostalgia, and count me in.

Are the players of today better than those of the fifties and sixties? Certainly. But in the Paradox of Progress, we know it is better and cannot explain why it feels worse. Blame it on the designated hitter, or the carousel of relief pitchers, or steroids, or the rise in strikeouts. But the best explanation is simply that we are older now. The unchanging game has changed, and so have we.

It has been a pleasant conceit to imagine that amid the continuing swirl of events a childhood game has been the constant of American life. For all our complaints today—and a widely held perception that the world used to be a better place and it must be someone's fault that it isn't any longer—it may likewise be argued that America is better than it ever was. To view our present state, in the game and in the land, with clarity is the calling of the past.

What was it like, to be alive then? That may seem simple for the autobiographer of a certain age (though it is not); it is a harder mission for the historian, to go beyond the recovery of accurate fact to recording an accuracy of feeling. For the oral historian, the mission is to present his interlocutor as he was in life, to go beyond stenography, as Peter Golenbock has done so brilliantly here. Like Larry Ritter, who may be said to have invented the genre of oral history, he has left behind mere transcription, like the Works Progress Administration interviews of the mid-1930s, to present word portraits more eloquent than voice.

He wakes the echoes.

John Thorn

Preface

When I was a junior at Dartmouth College, a book arrived for me, the sports editor of the Dartmouth daily newspaper. It was titled *The Glory of Their Times*, and it was a book of reminiscences of baseball players, famous and not so famous, who played in the 1910s and the 1920s. The author was a man by the name of Larry Ritter, who had spent five years driving 75,000 miles around the country with his reel-to-reel tape recorder to interview men like Rube Marquard, Tommy Leach, Davy Jones, and Sam Crawford, who played in the outfield beside Ty Cobb.

I started to read it, and immediately I was swept up, transported to a different time, an age when the likes of Cobb and Joe Jackson starred along with Walter Johnson and Christy Mathewson. To this day I think of *The Glory of Their Times* as the bible of baseball, and whenever I teach my course on baseball and American culture, I always include it in the required readings.

Inspired by *The Glory of Their Times*, as well as *Ball Four* by Jim Bouton and *The Boys of Summer* by Roger Kahn, in 1975 I published *Dynasty*, my bestselling history of the Yankees from 1949 to 1964. For that book I interviewed almost fifty former Yankees. After that I wrote oral histories of the Brooklyn Dodgers, the Boston Red Sox, the Chicago Cubs, the St. Louis Cardinals and Browns, and the New York Mets. For each book I interviewed dozens of players, executives, and journalists, using pieces of those interviews for the body of those books.

It is now the year 2021, fifty years since Larry published *The Glory of Their Times*. In the meantime many of the players I interviewed for my team histories have passed away, leaving me with hundreds of hours of tapes of our conversations about their teams and the national pastime.

My goal with *Whispers of the Gods* is to write a book that allows the next generation of players to tell their stories about their managers, teammates, and important moments. The book is dedicated to the men who mentored me while I was just getting started, Roger Kahn, Larry Ritter, Harold Rosenthal, Joel Oppenheimer, Jim Bouton, and Joe Flaherty, and to Jimmy Breslin and Pete Hamill, who were my writing heroes. You were the very best.

Jim Bouton

I thought, *Christ, I'll be able to throw forever. I have the right combination of guts, pitching when the chips are down. I'm better in big ball games.*

—Jim Bouton

$\mathcal{O}$ne of the joys of writing *Dynasty*, my history of the New York Yankees of the 1950s and early '60s was becoming close with pitcher Jim Bouton and his family. I was living in Englewood, New Jersey, as he did, and after our initial meeting we became like brothers. He and his wife, Bobbi, and I and my wife would go out, and before long we would babysit their three young children, Michael, David, and Laurie, whom everyone called Twink. Jim invited me to play on the CBS All-Star softball team starring Jim Jensen, and I ended up playing for CBS for six seasons, traveling the tristate area playing top semipro, police, fire, and charity teams. Jim and I raced our Fiats on the street and

Jim Bouton. National Baseball Hall of Fame

raced go-karts at amusement parks. I never won a race. One evening, he and Mike Kekich and I went to a local poorly lit high school gym, where I caught Kekich's ninety-mile-an-hour fastball and Jim's dancing knuckleball. In the summer of 1978, he invited me to come to Atlanta to watch him pitch a game against the Dodgers.

Jim Bouton: I was not considered a big prospect at all. I pitched for Boone Township High School and bloomed late. I hardly pitched at all as a junior in high school. I was small, about 5-foot-10, 145 pounds. I didn't develop until college.

My senior year in high school, I pitched in a semifinal game for the state [Michigan] championship. Maywood High School beat us 2–1 in 13 innings. They went on to win the [1957] state championship. After I lost in 13 innings, I pitched that summer for a team called the Chicago Yankees; strangely enough, no relationship to the real Yankees. We played about an eighty-five-game schedule, and I was one of four pitchers, and I learned a lot that summer. I got pretty good, so I played my freshman year at Western Michigan, and then I pitched for the Chicago Yankees again.

At the end of that summer, I pitched in a tournament in Battle Creek. I was the fourth pitcher. We had college phenoms like Jim Hansen, guys you don't know, but they were big names at the time. I pitched against the team that ended up winning it in double elimination, and I beat them 2–0, a two-hitter, and it was the only game they lost. It was the first time scouts really took an interest in me. Before that, they considered me too small, too thin, not enough fastball. I was seen as a gutsy pitcher but without enough stuff. But after this particular game, they started to take an interest in me. Six or seven clubs were talking about me signing a big bonus contract. This was the finals of the tournament, the best teams from all over the country played, so all the scouts were there.

I drove home right after the tournament was over, and all the scouts were saying, "We're going to call you." It was about a four-hour drive to my house. I got home. My dad was playing bridge.

"Hey Dad," I said, "I pitched a two-hitter in a tournament, and scouts are talking about paying me a bonus."

My dad said, "Two spades."

"No, I'm not kidding you, Dad. They're going to call any minute now. How much money should I tell them I'd sign for?"

Still not believing, he threw out a number.

"Tell them fifty thousand dollars," he said.

There had never been any interest in me before, he felt, so why should there be any interest in me now?

Two seconds later, the phone rings. It was a scout from the Philadelphia Phillies.

"Fifty thousand dollars," I told the scout.

"Dad, I told him $50,000."

He said, "What did he say?"

"He wants to fly me to Philadelphia for a workout."

At that point, my dad began to take it seriously.

I went to Detroit to work out. I flew to Philadelphia. In each case, they told me I was too small. Other teams: St. Louis, Cincinnati, never wrote back, never called. So now I'm going back to college. I was really disappointed.

My dad tried one more trick: the fake letter gambit. We wrote a form letter. "Dear blank. My son is prepared to sign a major league contract by Thanksgiving. If you're interested please have your bid in, otherwise you're not going to be able to sign him. Yours truly, George Bouton."

He sent the letter to twelve clubs, including the Yankees.

The Yankees, afraid of losing me to somebody, offered me $30,000 for three years, about $10,000 a year. I was signed by Art Stewart, who knew the talent in the Chicago area. I was the first guy he signed.

I played three years in the minor leagues. I had an Amarillo contract, and I was not expected to make the Yankees in '62. I was probably going to Richmond when I went to spring training with twelve other pitchers from the minor leagues. Our job was to get in the game for a look-see. And I got lucky.

The Yankees and the Cardinals were playing in St. Petersburg. I was supposed to pitch the ninth inning, and I did, and we tied it up, so I pitched the 10th inning, and then I pitched the 11th inning, and the 12th, until I finally lost it in the 13th on an error. I had pitched four innings without giving up a run, and because of that I got another opportunity. They gave me enough rope to hang myself. They gave me a couple more chances to pitch, and I did well again, and [Ralph] Houk finally gave me a start, and I pitched five or six innings, and because I had one of the best pitching records for a rookie, or anyone else, they kept me and Robin Roberts. They were going to keep one of us.

Roberts wasn't impressive in the spring or on the sidelines. Robin had to get into a game to show how impressive he was. The spring was for the young, hard-throwing kids.

The Yankees went north, and I pitched a couple of innings in relief, and I got a starting opportunity against the Washington Senators just before cutdown. And I pitched a shutout. It was the world's worst shutout. I walked seven guys and gave up seven hits. "You pitched a shutout, kid, but you wore out the whole bullpen," Houk told me afterward.

In spring training, they don't tell you until the last minute whether you're going to make the club. There were ten marginal guys who all have their bags packed, who have made the travel arrangements for their wives, and then they show up on the last day, and you hear, "Ralph Houk wants to see ya," and Ralph says, "You're not going north with the club." Or you'd be in front of your locker, and the clubhouse guy has packed everybody's bag to travel north but yours. That's how you knew you were going to the minors.

They cut Roberts and kept me. And I spent most of the year as a relief pitcher. [In 1962, Bouton had a 7–7 record with a 3.99 ERA.]

I didn't start regularly until the following year when Bill Stafford came down with a rash in Baltimore one day in May. Stafford broke out in hives. Just one of those freak things. I was only supposed to pitch in that one game, and I won, so I stayed in the rotation. It really didn't matter to me whether I started or not. At that point in my career, I was just happy to be there and do anything they wanted me to do.

Our pitching coach was Johnny Sain, and I thought Johnny was terrific. He was a great pitching coach and a fine person, mostly giving me confidence. One of the best things coaches can do to big league athletes is leave them alone. So many coaches exert negative influence on players. If there is no influence at all, it can be positive. [Manager] Ralph Houk and Sain—the best things they contributed was the fact that they didn't bug you too much. They just left the guys alone. They didn't hassle us on running. Didn't hassle us on curfew, didn't hassle us on Mickey Mouse shit that other coaches would bug guys about. For that reason alone, they were very good.

Sain was a good teacher, too. He would never say, "You got to stop doing this and got to start doing that." He would wean you over gradually to his ideas. You're talking about guys who have been successful all their lives in baseball. Even if you're unsuccessful in the big leagues, you're been successful all the way along the line. It's difficult to take a twenty-three-year-old and tell him, "Let's change everything around."

You're not inclined to want to do it. Sain had a way of looking at a pitcher and right away realizing what his strengths and weaknesses were, what his potential was.

And so I started in Baltimore, stayed in the rotation and won twenty-one games, and I remember thinking that I didn't think it would be this easy. I remember thinking I would be able to do this for years and years and years and I would be in the Hall of Fame.

The ball would fly out of my hand. It took a lot of energy to throw it, but I had never had a sore arm. Even though I was only 5-foot-10, I used to throw very, very hard. I thought, *Christ, I'll be able to throw forever. I have the right combination of guts, pitching when the chips are down. I'm better in big ball games.*

I had all the ingredients. I would wind up and the ball would literally fly out of my hand.

I was scheduled to pitch the second game of the '63 World Series against the Dodgers in LA. The night before, Phil Linz, Pepi, Tony Kubek, and I went down to Grauman's Chinese Theater and we bought a hideous Halloween mask at a theatrical makeup store. The mask was made by makeup artists, and it cost twenty dollars. It fit over your head and was hideous and

Ralph Houk. National Baseball Hall of Fame

looked absolutely real. Wearing the mask, I looked like a person who had been burned beyond recognition.

We took turns wearing the mask. There was a crowd around Grauman's Chinese Theater looking at the footprints and signatures on the Hollywood

Walk of Fame, and we'd go with our head down, looking at their feet, and then we'd raise our face to somebody, and they would always jump. The mask was so real looking they'd be embarrassed by their fright. They'd try to recover so as not to make me feel bad for my deformity. We also had headlines made up. Mine was, "Bouton's two hitter beats Drysdale 1–0."

I had the headline right. I just had the names wrong. We lost 1–0. Tommy Davis singled in a run in the first inning. Then nothing. Drysdale was very tough. He and Koufax, when they had their good days, nobody hit them. Actually, in the first game we scored a couple runs against Koufax. He beat us 5–2. If we had scored two runs in my game, I would have beaten Drysdale 2–1.

We were swept by the Dodgers.

Ralph Houk became the Yankees general manager in 1964, and Yogi became the manager. The morale of the team disintegrated all at once when Houk became the general manager. It was bad in '64 because of the way he treated us with our contracts. A lot of guys were unhappy with him, but I had the most trouble.

When I went to spring training in '64, I asked him for $20,000, double what I made in 1963. I thought an extra 10,000 was fair for my winning twenty-one games. This is where a lot of teams are penny-wise and pound-foolish. It's a false economy to have a crucial guy miss time over a few thousand dollars.

It was Ralph's first year as general manager. Evidently there was a profit-sharing plan. Every dollar he cheated a player out of, he'd get to keep half of it. So there are financial reasons for doing it. And Ralph wanted to establish himself as a tough guy. A $10,000 raise for winning twenty-one games? I didn't think that was outrageous. The young kids today . . . At any rate, he wouldn't give it to me, and I had to hold out. He was offering me a $5,000 raise until the week before spring training, and then he offered me $6,000 a week after spring training started, which was outrageous. We finally ended up settling for $18,500. But that was after I held out for a couple of weeks. He threatened to fine me a hundred dollars a day if I didn't sign.

I was young and scared and didn't think I had any choice, so I signed.

I came to hate the guy. I realized he had two faces. He would do whatever he felt he had to do. Perhaps he really didn't like me when he was the manager. Maybe he only liked me because I was a good player for him and he could get something out of me, but he didn't care for me as a person. He didn't care for people, otherwise why would he treat me like that when it came time to pay me? That's where I lost a tremendous amount of respect for Ralph.

The players also grumbled about Yogi, and this is what I couldn't understand: why the players didn't like Yogi. Except that Houk had been such a

Yogi Berra. Author collection

great manager. The players liked him so much, and they weren't able to accept anybody else. They weren't able to accept Yogi.

They were constantly talking behind Yogi's back. Yeah, it was terrible. "Oh, Yogi has no tact." "Did you hear what Yogi said at the meeting today?" "Jesus, Yogi doesn't give you a pat on the back." "Yogi isn't cracking down."

The worst complainers were Tony Kubek and Bobby Richardson. But it was practically the whole ball club. Even his worst critics can't tell me why Yogi was no good, which makes one conclude he must have been a good manager. And he was. I said it at the time. He knows strategy. He knows when to take a pitcher out of a ball game. What Yogi is not good at is holding a team meeting. He says things that makes guys laugh. He gives them reasons not to respect him. He's not a commanding figure like Ralph Houk or Freddy Hutchinson, and that gives you an opportunity to poke fun at him. Houk knew just what to say to each guy. He was a master psychologist. Yogi was very blunt, but a good man nevertheless and a good manager. We won the pennant with Yogi. How bad could he have been, for Christ sakes?

In 1964, we won it on memory and Mel Stottlemyre. [Mel was 9–3 with a 2.02 ERA as a rookie.] I had my second good season. You can't say you had your *last* good season when you only have two. When Mel Stottlemyre came up, I thought, *We will never get beat. The ball club will go on forever.*

But in the spring of 1964 after my holdout, my arm started to hurt me, and it bothered me until the All-Star break. I had only won about five games by the All-Star break in '64. I was 5–8.

Yogi never got on me. He'd say to me, "You'll be all right," and that was it. Which was good. It was one of the reasons Yogi was good. He didn't bug you. He knew my arm was bothering me, and he was hoping it would get better. It was a strange kind of soreness, not the conventional elbow or shoulder. It was a dull toothache in my bicep. I had strained a muscle way down next to the bone.

After the All-Star break, Yogi gave me one more start. I had had a couple of infected wisdom teeth pulled during the All-Star break, and when I came back I threw a shutout against California, and then I pitched again and threw another shutout, so he kept me in the rotation, and I won thirteen games the second half of the '64 season. I finished the year 18–13.

After we won the pennant in '64, Yogi was fired, and Houk brought in Johnny Keane from the Cardinals. Houk had played all those years behind Yogi, and I'm sure there was a certain amount of resentment. Also, Yogi was not Houk's choice. Houk was given the job at the same time Yogi was appointed manager. Houk considered it a promotion and he wasn't about to rock the boat. Yogi was part of the package. Houk had no choice in the matter. So even though we won the pennant under Yogi in '64, he wanted to get rid of Yogi and get his own man in there, Johnny Keane. Keane won the pennant in St. Louis. He was a class guy. Keane had been part of a winning organization for a long, long time. Keane had the reputation for building a team from the ground up. So Houk picked him. And he was available.

And Keane was absolutely the wrong guy. The players may not have respected Yogi, but at least they liked him. Keane they didn't respect or like. Johnny was too old for us and much too traditional. We had gotten into outrageous habits—training habits, lifestyle habits, like running around the roof of the Shoreham Hotel, like absolutely never coming in by curfew. During spring training, we hardly slept at all.

I remember Johnny Keane's first meeting in spring training.

"I'm Johnny Keane. We have a great ball club. I'm proud to be the manager of the Yankees. I've always considered this the greatest job in baseball. I'm here, and I'm going to let you guys play ball. I want you to do things your way because you've been successful. I'm not going to try to tell you guys how to play ball. You're men, and I'm going to leave you alone. You're not going to show me anything I haven't seen in my twenty-five years of managing baseball."

Okay fine. Two weeks of spring training go by, and we're losing. We're about one and eight, and Keane starts hanging around the hotel, and nobody is coming in. Guys were drunk in bars, staggering around the hotel. Guys were overweight. We would come to practice in the morning with alcohol coming out of every pore of our bodies, and I want to emphasize *our* bodies. Include me in on this so we don't have any doubts.

John held another meeting. "Fellas," he said, "I told you the first day that I had seen just about everything in my years of baseball. But men, I was wrong. There are about five or you who have gotten into some careless habits. You are acting very carelessly. And I would like to see a stop to that."

I can remember sitting at the bar with guys, and I would say, "Should we have another round?"

"I don't know," they would say. "It's awfully careless of us. Should we be so careless as to have another round?"

"Yeah, let's."

We still didn't keep any hours at all. We stayed out until two or three in the morning. At times, we stayed out all night. It had always worked out for us before. We had always won pennants before.

A couple weeks later, Keane held another meeting, and he told us there were about *fifteen* of us who were getting careless.

Christ, we had never needed spring training before. Spring training was just so they knew we were going to show up for the first regular season game, so maybe we would practice plane rides and bus rides a little before the season started.

We really didn't need spring training. Yes, there was a certain amount of getting in shape, but when you see Moose Skowron go five for six in the first spring training game, you know spring training is for the other guys. It was for Joe DeMaestri and the other bench guys. On the third day of spring training, Skowron rifled another hit to right field, and DeMaestri said, "One more hit, Moose, and you'll be hitting eleven fifty-three." That's the way spring training had always been for us. We had never kept hours in the past. We figured that Bobby Richardson was going to get in early for the rest of us.

But Keane couldn't tolerate this, and we weren't winning in spring training, which also had never been important in the past. If we won in spring training, we won. If we didn't, we didn't. It didn't matter. We were going to win the pennant regardless.

Keane held a meeting at the end of spring training, and the number was up to *twenty-three* guys who had been careless. We were all sitting there snickering with grins on our faces, and Bobby Richardson and Tony Kubek knew they were the only ones on the club who were not careless.

Keane became angry. We all wanted Ralph Houk to manage us. Guys were complaining now. Where before they were complaining about Yogi once in a while, they were complaining to Houk every day. It was terrible. And John did not have the good humor to laugh it off.

John didn't have the good past associations that Yogi had. We might laugh at Yogi, but we really couldn't get pissed off at him. Keane you got pissed off at right away. And John was a very religious man. Our behavior upset his moral value. Yogi didn't like it because he thought we'd play better. He didn't care about the rest of it. But it was an affront to Keane's sensibilities as well as what he thought it was doing to us on the ball field. John didn't have the patience and flexibility to deal with it. He was an older man.

We'd play tricks on him. We were always talking about what Squeaky did today. I remember we were standing in the lobby, and John walked in and nodded his head.

"Good afternoon, John," we said.

"Good afternoon, gentlemen of the jury."

He knew he was on trial.

And then it seemed that twelve guys got old. In '65, there were a lot of injuries. That was the year Mantle and Maris were playing tunes on their hamstrings every other week. John thought the players were babying themselves too much. He would always try to get Mickey to play in the game.

"How's the leg, Mickey?" he would ask.

I would make up a conversation. I would be Mickey, and I'd be Johnny Keane. Mickey used to get a kick out of it.

"How is your leg, Mickey?"

"Not too good, skip. It's broken in four places."

"Well, I know, but how does it feel?"

"It feels all right. I just can't set the bones in time. I only have an hour before the game starts."

"See if you can get it set by then. We can sure use you out there. What about your back?"

"My back fell clean off."

"What the hell. Can you get another back? We can get another back for you by game time."

"That would be all right. I guess I can play."

"Good, Mick. I know you can play."

Keane played a lot of the guys who were injured. He made Maris play when he was injured, and he shouldn't have. Of course, Houk backed Keane on that. I pitched when I shouldn't have. It was the year when my legs got heavy and my arm started hurting me.

In '64, my arm had bothered me the first half of the season, and then I snapped out of it. In '65, the pain never went away. Keane had seen the turnabout the year before, that I had won thirteen games the second half, and he figured I'd do that again, and I never did. My arm trouble never went away. [Jim finished 1965 with 4–18 with a 4.82 ERA.]

I went from being a star to a less-than-winning pitcher in '65, and it affected my personality. I'm a very intense person anyway. To have me suddenly not be able to win at all and have a sore arm made me very difficult to live with. Plus, when a player is losing and not contributing, you're not willing to go that extra step in accepting others, and I was very difficult to get along with. That year, a lot of guys had difficulty getting along with each other. There was a tremendous amount of tension on the ball club.

All the time. It was an unhappy clubhouse.

I didn't have any particular trouble with Keane, but Joe Pepitone was really having trouble with him, and so was Clete Boyer, and so were Maris and Mantle. Everybody was always in a bad mood. I can't remember laughing and smiling and joking like we used to do. Everybody was rubbing each other the wrong way. It was an incredibly difficult period for all of us.

Maris and Boyer and I had deep resentments of each other. Mostly because Maris was deeply resentful of the press and the fans, and during the same period I had a good relationship with the writers and the fans. The contrast was always there for them to see, and so it accelerated our other differences that we had.

They hated Lenny Shecter, and I would have dinner with Lenny. They hated Steve Jacobson, and I would have dinner with Steve Jacobson. These writers were my friends. Fans would say to the other Yankees, "Why won't you sign autographs? Jim Bouton signs autographs?" It was a constant reminder. I don't want to put blame on Boyer and Maris, because it was as much my fault as anybody's. Maris had hit 61 home runs, and now he was sitting out with a pulled hamstring muscle, and I had won 21 games, and I couldn't even throw the ball. Christ, this was our job. This was our living, our livelihood, our future, and we weren't able to do it. God damn, it was very frightening. You didn't know what the hell the future was going to hold for you.

[The Yankees finished the 1965 season 77–85, twenty-five games behind the Minnesota Twins. In 1966, the Yankees fell to 70–89, tenth in the American League. Johnny Keane was fired after the first twenty games. His record was 4–16. The Yankees fell out of contention for the next decade.]

• 2 •

Ed Froelich

"You tell those people for Baby"—he always called himself
Baby—"that Baby says they're full of crap right up to their eyes.
I may be dumb, but I'm not that dumb."

—Ed Froelich, quoting Babe Ruth

*E*ddie Froelich was the trainer for Joe Mc-
Carthy when Marse Joe was manager for the
Chicago Cubs, the New York Yankees, and
the Boston Red Sox. He was also trainer
for the Brooklyn Dodgers when Babe Ruth
was hired by owner Larry MacPhail in 1938
to be a coach. In an interview in 1989, four
years before he died, Ed Froelich remembered the Babe, both in New York and in
Brooklyn. Froelich's stories recall the greatness of the man they called the Bambino and
the Sultan of Swat and serve to remind fans
of the excitement and joy that he brought to
America's pastime.

Joe McCarthy. National Baseball
Hall of Fame

Ruth, according to Froelich and just
about anyone else who ever saw him play,
was as colorful as any ballplayer in the
game's history on and off the field. Everyone loved the Babe, because he was
outgoing and fun-loving and because he was honest and forthright. Ask Babe
a question, and he'd give you a straight answer.

According to Froelich, the myth that he had pointed to center field
before hitting his famous home run in the 1932 World Series made Ruth un-

12

comfortable. Ruth sneered at the legend because it wasn't true and because he had too much respect for Chicago Cubs pitcher Charlie Root to perpetuate it.

Froelich recalls the Babe's greatness, including an incident in Brooklyn that gives some insight into just how great a pitcher Babe Ruth had been.

Eddie Froelich: The Yankees were in Philadelphia to play an important series with the Philadelphia A's, and a bunch of players said, "Aw nuts, we've been keeping our noses to the grindstone. We're going out and relax."

So a whole slew of guys went out and relaxed, and Ruth was one of them. They went to this whorehouse in Philadelphia, and there was music and girls and whiskey and food, everything you might want for a nice party. Everyone had a nice time, and now it was 1:30 in the morning, and finally someone said, "Time to go home."

Before long, everybody started trooping out of the place.

"Are you coming, Babe?" he was asked.

"No," said Ruth. "I'll catch you later."

The next day, the players were on the way to the ballpark. They had to drive down the same street as the house where they had partied the night before, and as they were going to the park, just as they passed the house, out came Babe.

Waite Hoyt, the great pitcher, was wondering what kind of condition Babe would be in to play that afternoon.

"All he did," Hoyt said, "was hit three home runs and he missed the fourth one by about two inches."

Ruth used to tell pitchers he was worried about only one thing. He said he was afraid of hitting a line drive back to the box and killing someone. He would tell the batting practice pitchers, "Don't pitch me outside. I don't want to hurt anyone." If he had hit a pitcher, he would have disabled him at best, killed him at worst.

Babe's feats were so well known that the term *Ruthian* has become part of the language. Every once in a while, Ruth would get under the ball when he swung, and he would hit the world's most towering pop-up. I swear, and this was no optical illusion, that he would hit a pop-up, and he would be pulling into second base as it came down. And he wouldn't be running hard. The fielders would look at each other and say, "Who wants it?" Many a time, no one wanted the damn thing. And sometimes nobody would catch it, and he'd end up with an infield double.

I remember it was 1938, and I was trainer for the Brooklyn Dodgers. Dodger owner Larry MacPhail had hired Ruth to be a Dodger coach. What he was supposed to be, actually, was a draw. It was in his contract that he had to take batting practice every day before the game to hit for the crowd.

Babe Ruth. National Baseball Hall of Fame

It used to be something to watch him take batting practice. When Babe stepped into the batter's box, everything on that ball field stopped. Some guys were throwing on the sidelines, others were playing pepper, but when the Babe got up, it all came to a halt. The King had just walked into the batter's box.

I remember a day at the Polo Grounds. It was the Fourth of July and the park was jammed. You couldn't get another person in with a shoehorn.

Ruth walked up to hit in batting practice, and he hit eight consecutive pitches into the right field stands beginning first with the right field foul line, moving over a few feet with each successive hit and finishing over the 440-foot sign. Then to put the frosting on the cake, he swung his bat with one hand and hammered one into the stands along the foul line. He tipped his cap and walked away. The place went into an uproar.

Have you seen films of Babe hitting? He had his ass to the pitcher, and he would only be looking at him with the corner of his right eye. This is a direct contradiction to the theory that you see something better if you look at it with both eyes. If I were ever going to coach a hitter, I would tell him to have both eyes on the pitcher. Stan Musial did that. Not Ruth. And Babe had a dip in his swing, a little hitch, and if you advised a batter, you'd tell him he could never hit with a hitch. And for most people, this is true. But such advice is for the ordinary person. When you're Babe Ruth, the ordinary doesn't apply.

With the Dodgers, Babe did something that stands out in my mind and will as long as I live. Ruth had been a pitcher and a great one. His record was 94 wins and 46 losses, better than a .667 percentage. He held the consecutive scoreless inning record in the World Series until Whitey Ford broke it in the sixties.

The Babe was very, very proud of his pitching, believe me. The fellows on the Dodgers used to kid him a little bit.

"Hey Babe," they'd say, "what kind of pitcher were you?"

"If I was pitching," Babe would say, "be glad you didn't have to hit against me because I would have stuck the ball up your ass."

This went on, and finally Babe came in to me one day and said, "One of these days, Doc, these guys are going to get me just mad enough that I'll get my arm in shape, and I'll pitch some batting practice against these bastards."

A few days later, he came in again, and he said, "Well, I've had enough of this crap. Beginning tomorrow, I'm going to start getting my arm in shape. I want you to help me."

"Okay," I said

"That means getting here at eight in the morning before anybody else."

I said again, "Okay."

So the Babe came out and threw for about a week, and one day after he had thrown, he came in and said, "The old hose feels pretty good, and now I'm laying in the weeds waiting for some of these guys to pop off."

A couple days later, one of them did pop off.

"I'll pitch batting practice any time you want," Ruth told him.

"When?" he was asked.

"Any time you say."

"How about tomorrow?"

"Okay," Babe said.

The next day, four of them came out to hit. There were Dolf Camilli, Ernie Koy, Babe Phelps, and I can't remember the fourth one, though it might have been Cookie Lavagetto.

Ruth pitched batting practice for about ten minutes, and only ten balls left the batting cage. Everything else was either a foul ball or a strike that went by them.

When it was over, I asked Phelps what Babe was throwing.

"I never saw anything like that before," Phelps said. "He was moving the ball every which way it's possible to move the ball, down and in, down and out, up and in, and up and out. He was throwing a fastball that hopped, and he threw an overhand fastball that sunk." He said, "It looks like a spitter, but he wasn't wetting the ball. It was the darnedest thing I ever saw."

A couple days later I was talking with Ruth.

"Babe," I said, "the guys are talking about the overhand fastball that you made sink like a spitter."

Ruth had a kind of funny laugh. He made the sound of *zzzzzzzzz*'s when he laughed.

"You know what I was doing with the ball?" he said.

"No," I said, and he showed me.

He threw an overhand fastball with his thumb curled underneath the ball.

"I make it act like a spitter," he said.

After that day of batting practice, there was no more ribbing him about his pitching.

Like I said, when Babe joined the Dodgers, he had been away from baseball full-time for four years, and when the Babe started to swing the bat again, he had some aches and pains. He would be in the training room every day.

We got talking one day. I said, "Babe, a lot of people in Chicago still say that you pointed toward the center field bleachers before you hit that home run out there."

"Doc," he said, "can you hear me?"

"Yes," I said.

A little louder he said, "Can you hear me, Doc?"

"Yes," I said.

"Can you hear me good?"

"Yes."

"You tell those people for Baby"—he always called himself Baby—"that Baby says they're full of crap right up to their eyes. I may be dumb, but I'm not that dumb. I'm going to point to the center field bleachers with a barracuda like Root out there? The next pitch they'd be picking out of my ear with a pair of tweezers."

Babe Ruth. Author collection

He said one final word: "No."

Root said he never pointed and so did Gabby Hartnett, the Cubs catcher, and so did the umpire. So what did happen? Ruth was at the plate, and the Cubs bench was calling him every obscene name they could think of. He had his bat on his shoulder, and Root threw a strike, and the Babe took it with his bat on his shoulder, and he got another blast from the Cubs bench.

With his bat on his shoulder, Ruth lifted the pointer finger of his right hand off the bat as if to say, "Okay, that's one."

Root pitched again, and Babe took it, and it was strike two, and he got another blast from the Cubs.

Ruth looked over to the Cubs dugout, raised two fingers of his right hand off the bat, signaled, "Okay, that's two."

Root pitched again, and Ruth hit the ball off the top of the ticket office in Wrigley Field's center field bleachers.

Have you ever seen a photograph of Ruth pointing? At the World Series, the place is swarming with photographers. You'd think one would have gotten the picture, but no.

As a rule, Babe didn't hit the ball into center field. Almost never. Would he be pointing to a spot where he almost never hit the ball? Doesn't make sense. But see, it's a legend. People like to believe in fantasy, even newspaper reporters. After the game, Grantland Rice and all the rest of the New York newspapermen were around in the clubhouse, and Rice said, "Babe, damn if it didn't look like you pointed when you hit the ball."

"The hell I did," Ruth said.

That's all he said. And the newspapermen created a legend from that.

Babe Ruth was a fabulous, fabulous person. God makes a Babe. You can't teach someone to play like he could.

· 3 ·

Marty Marion

I was playing shortstop, and as Ted was coming around second base he gave me a wink, and he said, "Kid, don't you wish you could hit like that?"

—Marty Marion

*M*arty Marion, eight times the National League's All-Star shortstop, joined the St. Louis Cardinals in 1940, as the Gashouse Gang era was ending. He joined Stan Musial, Enos Slaughter, and the Cooper brothers, Mort and Walker, in leading the Cards to the most successful era in the club's history. The Cards, built by general manager Branch Rickey, won pennants in 1942, 1943, 1944, and 1946 and won the World Series in '42, '44, and '46. Marion was named the most valuable player in the National League in 1944. He was the first shortstop to win the award.

Marty Marion. Author collection

Marion, who had an astute business mind, was a tough negotiator when fighting for his salary. When I visited him, he was living in a palatial home that looked like Tara from *Gone with the Wind*.

When Jackie Robinson came to the Dodgers in 1947, the southerners on the Cardinals, including Marion, Enos Slaughter, Terry Moore, and Harry

Walker, were accused of fomenting talk of a strike if Robinson played. As you will see, Marion stoutly has denied that was true.

His playing career ended after the 1950 season, becoming a manager for the St. Louis Cardinals, St. Louis Browns, and Chicago White Sox.

He died on March 15, 2011, in Ladue, Missouri, at the age of ninety-four.

Marty Marion: I was born in Richburg, South Carolina, in 1916. My daddy was a cotton farmer. He had to stay home and work until he could send his sisters to college. He moved to Atlanta when I was just a baby, two years old, and I was raised in Atlanta.

We hated the yankees. I don't mean the baseball Yankees. Everybody who lived up north was a yankee. We were very opinionated. We didn't like anyone who wasn't a southerner. But that has changed. Atlanta is quite a city now.

My brother Johnny was three years older, and at one time he played with the Washington Senators. When I graduated from high school my brother was a player for Chattanooga, Tennessee, in the Southern League. He arranged for me to come to Chattanooga to work out with the Lookouts, a Washington farm club.

I drove up in a Model A Ford. It was black with red wheels. My daddy bought it for $75. I wish I still had it. I went to Chattanooga, and Calvin Griffith, who was running the Lookout baseball team, decided he'd like to sign me.

They gave me $500 to sign. Oh, that was big money. I was there three or four days when Chattanooga went on a road trip. I was just a kid, and nobody told me what to do, and I got in the car and drove back home to see my sweetheart, my wife today. Two or three days later, I drove back to Chattanooga. The team hadn't gotten back to town yet, so I walked into the office.

"Why did you leave town?" Cal Griffith wanted to know.

"Well, nobody told me to stay," I said. "Nobody told me nothing."

"We're going to release you," said Griffith.

He handed me my release.

After I became a pretty famous major leaguer, every time I'd see Calvin, I'd say to him, "Cal, remember when you released me?"

Everybody in Atlanta knew I was a good high school player, and the Cardinals were holding a tryout camp in Rome, Georgia, so I was advised, "Marty, why don't you go up to the tryout camp?"

I played in an intersquad game. I played about three innings, and the scouts called me over right quick.

"Kid, how would you like to make a trip to St. Louis?" I was asked.

"I have to go back and ask my mommy and daddy," I said.

I went back home, and pretty soon I was getting telegrams from Branch Rickey in St. Louis saying the Cardinals would pay my expenses. There was another boy in camp, Johnny Eckles, and they wanted him to come, too, so Johnny and I got on the train.

We dressed and worked out before the last couple games of the 1935 season, and we saw Phil Cavarretta hit a home run off Paul Dean to beat the Cardinals 1–0 to win the pennant. Mr. Rickey called us up to his office after we worked out. I could tell he was more interested in Johnny than he was in me. But Johnny and I on the train made a pact that we weren't going to sign unless both of us signed. We started dickering with Mr. Rickey, and we didn't sign. We came on back home to Atlanta.

[Younger brother] Frank Rickey came down that winter and started taking us out to dinner and entertaining us. He was telling us what the Cardinals could do for us. I was a pretty good businessman, and I came up with a deal that Johnny agreed to: we would get a four-year con-

Branch Rickey. Author collection

tract. This was 1935. Nobody had heard of something like this. The first year, we'd make $125 a month no matter where they sent us. The second year, we'd get $175 a month. The third year, we'd make $3,000 a year, and the fourth year, we'd make $5,000, which was more than the major league minimum. And we were just high school kids! I had already been fired once and I hadn't even played a game.

I was eighteen, and I wrote what they promised us on an envelope.

I began play in Huntington, West Virginia, a nice little town. It was my first year away from home. I was the only one who made it to the major leagues from that team. I'll never forget the first notice I ever got as a player: Dukes Rigly, the sports editor of the *Huntington Times*, said, "That kid Marty Marion playing shortstop looks like a girl just learning how to wear her first pair of high heel slippers."

And then before the year was out, he said I was the best prospect in the whole league.

The next year, I went to Rochester, Triple A. I spent three years there learning to play shortstop. They released Johnny Eckles during the fourth year of our contract.

"They can't do that," I said. "We have a contract."

Mr. Rickey called Johnny and me into his office.

"What do you mean, I can't fire you?" Rickey said. "I can fire Joe Medwick. I can fire Johnny Mize. I can fire anybody I want to."

"Yeah, Mr. Rickey," I said, "but you can't fire us. We got a contract. The piece of paper I wrote it down on promised this to us."

Judge Landis, the baseball commissioner, heard about it, and he called Johnny and me to Clearwater, where he stayed in a big ole wooden hotel over there [the Belleview-Biltmore]. He was sitting on the front porch, leaning up against the banister.

"What did Mr. Rickey promise you?" he asked. "Do you have any proof."

"I wrote it down," I said. "He promised we would have a four-year contract."

I told him the details.

"Thank you, boys," he said.

He called Mr. Rickey over there, and the Cardinals had to re-sign Johnny for $5,000. They sent him to Pocatello, Idaho, and he wound up as the Cardinals batting practice pitcher. After that year, they released him, and he was gone.

Rickey sent me back to Rochester in 1939.

"I can play shortstop a lot better than the guys you've got," I told Mr. Rickey.

"Well," he said, "you can go back to Rochester."

They were playing Sammy Baugh at shortstop, and he was a pretty good baseball player. Later, he became a very famous football player with the Washington Redskins.

"I knew I was never going to make that baseball team with Marty Marion there," he later said.

I was sitting on the bench while Sammy was playing shortstop, just sitting there doing nothing, when our manager, Ray Blades, said, "Marty, you have a good arm. Maybe I'll make a pitcher out of you. Go to the sidelines and warm up. You have a good fastball. Let me see your curveball."

I gave him my best curveball.

"Get back to shortstop," he said.

That was the end of that. Ray Blades and I came up to the Cardinals in 1940, and I stayed. I was living on cloud nine just being a kid with the Cardinals.

Ray was a very serious man. In that I came up from the South, I would call someone older than me "Sir." I always called Ray "Sir."

"Don't call me Sir," Ray said. "Call me Blades."

So I called him Mr. Blades.

"Don't call me Mr. Blades."

He wanted me to call him Ray. I suppose he took a liking to me because of my being a young kid. One time, we were going bad, so he batted me third.

"Hell," he said, "you're hitting better than anyone else on the club."

That didn't last too long. We had Johnny Mize, Walker Cooper, Enos Slaughter, Terry Moore, and Harry Walker.

In June [1940], our owner, Mr. Breadon, fired Ray, and Billy Southworth came in. Billy was a happy-go-lucky guy whose motto was "You can catch more flies with honey than you can with vinegar." He tried to make peace with everybody. He was a good manager.

What I remember most about Southworth was how he kept hunting for his son after he was killed in the army. His whole life was around that boy, Billy Jr. He was a handsome boy, and many times the kid would come into the clubhouse dressed in his soldier's outfit.

He was a pilot, and he was lost in action. As manager of the Cardinals, Billy had some influence, and he would go and talk to all the people in the army. After the boy died, Billy went through hell. Gosh, that was sad.

Billy had the theory of trying to make you happy. The only run-in I ever had with him came after he took me out for a pinch hitter in a game. He was in the habit of doing that, and I got tired of it. We were winning, and I got to be a pretty good hitter, so one day he took me out, and I came back to the bench, and I said, "Billy, if this guy can hit for me, he can field for me too. I'm tired of you taking me out for a pinch hitter."

I stormed into the clubhouse. When the game was over, he came over to my locker and put his arm around me.

"You know," he said, "we've been together for a long time."

He knew how to handle me. He didn't get mad at me. His theory of getting more flies with honey always worked for Bill. He didn't say he was sorry. Oh no. He just consoled me and put his arm around me. But as long as he was there, he never took me out for another pinch hitter again.

Branch Rickey was our general manager. He was a great baseball man from what he did through his career. But one thing about him, no matter how well you did on the baseball field, you got a two-page letter the next year for your contract. He wrote a beautiful letter, and he'd always cut your salary. You were lucky to get your original salary back.

"Mr. Rickey," I told him. "I ain't gonna play for that. I don't care what you say."

Stan Musial came the last three weeks of the '41 season. We weren't impressed much with Stan, even in 1942. Stan played very little against left-handers. Coaker Triplett hit against the left-handers. At first, Stan was just another ballplayer, but as the years went on, he became very important.

Stan Musial. National Baseball Hall of Fame

Mr. Rickey thought that Erv Dusak was a better ballplayer than Stan. Four-Sack Dusak they called him. He was a nice man, but he never had the talent Stan had. He was a good prospect with power, but he never did materialize.

My first year with the Cardinals, Johnny Mize and Joe Medwick were there. They were jealous of each other. I'd be sitting next to Medwick, and if

Mize got a cheap hit, Joe would say, "They never give me those cheap hits." Same thing with Mize. He'd say, "They never give me those cheap hits."

Mr. Rickey finally traded both of them. Mize went to the Giants. Ol' John. He was from Demerest, Georgia, and all he wanted to do was rub down his bats. He had forty-two bats in the bat rack, and I had two. All John cared about was hitting, and he could hit that ball. He had a lot of power to left center. He had forty-two bats. I counted them one time. I would go to the team secretary and say, "I need some bats."

Well, they got me two. But Mize got all he wanted.

Medwick went to the Dodgers. Good ol' Joe had a mean streak in him. During batting practice, he used to see if he could hit the pitcher. We didn't have screens. He'd hit line drives off the pitcher's shins, a line drive through the box, and he'd just laugh. Later in life, Joe mellowed. After he got to the Dodgers, everybody loved Joe. He was a has-been then. It's funny what a nice guy you can be when you're hitting .250 but what a son of a bitch you are when you're hitting .350. That's baseball.

I'll never forget the time we were playing the Dodgers and Medwick was on first base, and he was stealing. I don't know why, because he couldn't run, but he slid into me at second base, and he kicked me with his spikes. I was tagging him, so I reached over and slapped him in the face with my glove. Joe hardly got off the ground, when everyone on the Cardinals went on top of him. Dixie Walker was screaming, "My leg. My leg got caught." He was on the bottom of the pile. The next day in the New York paper, there was a big picture of the fight—it wasn't much of a fight—I'm standing on the bag looking down, and I had started the whole thing.

The Cardinals had so many players in the minor leagues that they could afford to trade players like Mize and Medwick. Mr. Rickey always believed in trading a player at the peak of his career, not when he was going down. Oh, we kept our bags packed all the time. They would say to us, "If you don't do good, they're going to send you to Rochester." Or Columbus. You never thought you were so good that you couldn't be replaced. You can be replaced.

In '42, Stan was just a part of the great team we had, and then in '43 he busted out and went into the army, and he then went on to become a big star and make $100,000.

Our biggest rivalry was with the Brooklyn Dodgers. The Cardinal–Dodger rivalry was friendly. Their manager was Leo Durocher, and he was not a nice man. But we loved Leo. You talk about the time Leo stole Babe Ruth's watch. Well, Walker Cooper had a watch, and every time we'd get in an argument with the Dodgers, Walker would wave his watch at Leo.

"Leo," Walker would say. "Look at this watch. It's Babe Ruth's watch."

We could be vicious, too. The reason our rivalry was so intense was that we battled the Dodgers every year for the pennant.

Leo had his pitchers throw at us. Everybody threw at us, but we threw at them, too. That was no sacred cow. We'd say, "You're going down. Get ready." And any time we went down, the next guy up for them went down, too, real quick. If you never wanted to lose respect from your own players, you didn't let anyone knock down your players without retaliating. Now it's against the law, but they still do it.

Harry Brecheen was the worst of them all. He had a habit every time he threw the ball and knocked somebody down, when the ball was halfway there he'd holler, "Look out. Look out." Oh yeah, he'd apologize to everybody for throwing at them.

We had a tough, rugged ball club. We'd fight you over anything.

One time, Mickey Owen was catching for the Dodgers, and Walker Cooper hit a ground ball, and he stepped on the Dodger first baseman. Owen ran down the first base line backing up the play, and after Cooper stepped on the first baseman, Mickey ran and jumped on Walker's back, and Cooper flipped him over real quick.

"I ain't gonna do that again," Owen said.

We didn't play dirty, but if you wanted to play dirty, we could play dirty.

The dueling match of the whole season was Mort Cooper against Whitlow Wyatt. Every time they faced each other, the score would be 1–0. Cooper was one of our best pitchers, but he was a rounder, didn't take good care of himself. When he first came up, he had a good fastball but nothing else and he was a little wild. Then he came up with a forkball and a change of speeds, and he gained control and a lot of confidence. He had a good team in back of him. Mort loved me.

"Marty," he used to say, "you and the double play are my best friends."

Mort would knock you down. His brother Walker was our catcher. Walker would say, "Mort, knock him down. I'll get him before he gets to you." And I guarantee you, he would, too. The Cooper boys were good. The year I won the Most Valuable Player in 1944, the Cooper boys were in their glory. Mr. Breadon sent me a contract, but I wouldn't sign it. He said, "Marty, I promised the Cooper boys they would be the highest-paid players on the team."

"I don't care," I said. "I ain't gonna play for that. I want $15,000."

That was more than the Cooper boys were making.

"All you have to do is call them and give them more money," I said.

During most of my time with the Cardinals I did most of my business with Mr. Breadon rather than Mr. Rickey. Mr. Breadon was a businessman who loved baseball, and he always liked me, even though I used to give him trouble contract-wise. I'd go into his office and sit down and talk with him, and he was always drinking that damn milk and eating crackers. He had a very bad stomach. He was always nervous.

I signed for more than they did. Mr. Breadon called them into his office and offered them the same as he had given me, but they weren't satisfied with that, and they went on strike. They didn't suit up. After they both got a raise, Mort bought me a new hat.

"You got me a raise," he said.

The Cooper brothers were the backbone of our Cardinals team. They were very good. But no way would I go out with them. We had cliques on the club. The Coopers and Johnny Beazley and Ernie White and Whitey Kurowki and Max Lanier all loved to drink beer and play cards. They always had a card game going in the hotel room. The guys who didn't drink and play cards were me, Harry Walker, Howie Pollet, Harry Brecheen, and Stan. They called us "college kids" even though none of us went to college. We were the "nice" kids. We weren't the tough guys on the block.

When they went to the hotel to play cards, we went to the movies. I would sometimes sit and watch them play. Finally, they had to stop. Mr. Dyer [the manager] had to ban playing cards because when you play cards, the loser is always the guy who can least afford to lose. The front office was getting complaints from the wives at home, so they must have been playing for some pretty good stakes. I never gambled in my life, so I didn't play cards.

Hell, they used to play pinochle in the clubhouse before the game. Dyer had to stop that, too. They weren't rowdy, but we called them "the mean bunch."

Sportsman's Park was a small ballpark. Only 42,000 could sit out there, and boy, we didn't fill it up much. One year we drew 200,000 fans. Baseball just wasn't all that popular at that time. You had two teams in St. Louis, the Cardinals and the Browns, and that divided up the town a little bit. The one team that was drawing was the Yankees with Ruth. The Babe packed them in. But we didn't draw. Hell, when you came to play for the Cardinals, $5,000 was a big salary. When Whitey Kurowski came, his first year he made $2,800.

St. Louis was a nice town, a friendly town, but it wasn't particularly glad to have ballplayers. Baseball players didn't have a good reputation, so when you'd go to rent a house, a lot of people would refuse. They thought we were drunkards. They thought baseball players were rowdy. When my grandfather, a Methodist minister, found out I was going to play baseball for a living, he liked to have gone crazy.

"They are just a bunch of ruffians," he said.

But even a bunch of barbers have ruffians. We were not highly regarded in the neighborhood, though the kids loved us. The grown people didn't. Ballplayers weren't the big heroes that they are today. Baseball has come a long way in that respect. They make more money, too, and that helps.

We played the Yankees in the '42 World Series. We had to win the final game of the season to get there. I remember going into the clubhouse that last day, and I was walking around bragging about getting the winning share of the World Series money.

"I read in the paper if we won," I said, "our share will be $6,192."

Terry Moore, our captain, was our leader. We respected Terry.

"Marty," he said, "don't talk like that. It's a jinx."

"The hell it is," I said.

Nobody talks about Terry. He taught me one thing in life. He said when he came to the big leagues, he got in a fight with a guy, and while he was asking a question, the guy popped him.

"Pop first and ask questions later," he advised me." He always told us, "If you're going to do something, do it fast. Don't wait and talk to him."

Terry was a loveable person. Harry Walker, ol' Needle Nose, named his son after Terry. He was a well-respected person on the Cardinal team, but nobody ever wrote a lot about Terry. He was just a good steady ballplayer, but one of the greatest center fielders you ever wanted to see play. He liked everyone. Everyone loved Terry. He was the kind of player who was in the background but meant a lot to the other players. But he never got the publicity that Enos got, that Medwick got.

The Yankees beat us in the first game [of the 1942 World Series], and we then beat them four straight. In the ninth inning of the final game, we picked Joe Gordon off second base. Jerry Priddy was the hitter, and it was a bunting situation. Gordon broke too far, and Walker Cooper threw the ball down to second, and Joe was out. It happens every day if a guy gets too far off second base. Gordon tried to scramble back, and without saying a word he dusted himself off and walked off.

It was a thrill to play in Yankee Stadium. The crowd for the last game at Yankee Stadium was 69,000. It was just awesome. The House that Ruth Built. It felt like you were in a mammoth arena. You felt you wanted to do better than you really can. Playing in Yankee Stadium gave you the feeling that you were important. There never was a stadium I'd ever been in that awed you like walking into Yankee Stadium.

In that final game Johnny Beazley held the Yankees to two runs. It was 2–2 in the ninth when Whitey Kurowski hit a ball down the line that went into the stands.

We won, but we weren't a club to jump up and down and scream and pour champagne on you. In fact, the only thing we ever had was a Coke. We didn't celebrate. We shook hands and patted everybody on the back, took off the uniform, and went home. We were not an emotional team at all. I can never remember shaking anybody's hand after coming into the dugout after getting a big hit. Never.

So, we won that last World Series game like it was just another game. Everyone was happy, and we won our $6,192, which was more than we made all year. My salary was $5,000, and it went up by $1,000 every year. Mr. Breadon and Mr. Rickey didn't have any money. Think about drawing 300,000 people, no television rights, if we got $100,000 for radio rights that was big, and at concessions a Coke was five cents and a hot dog was a dime. Back in those days, they didn't have any money.

Mr. Rickey left after the 1942 season, and I was kind of glad. I figured I could get more money from Mr. Breadon, which I did. We didn't appreciate Mr. Rickey. We always talked bad about him behind his back.

"He's a so and so old man, and he's so rich."

In a way, he was kind of a villain. He was a demon. He was the law. He was keeping us from getting the money. He was the guy who could send you back to Rochester.

With Mr. Rickey gone, no longer were there two pages of silver-tongued oratory telling you how lousy you were and giving you a cut in salary. All Mr. Breadon would say was, "Dear Marty. Please sign the contract and return it. See you in the spring."

I can remember when I heard that the Japanese had attacked Pearl Harbor. I was sitting in my ol' Chevrolet car listening to the radio in the front yard of the driveway of this farm in South Carolina. We were getting ready to go on a shopping trip to Anderson, South Carolina. It was in the wintertime.

Uh oh, I thought, *everything is going to break loose.* By 1943, the war was on, and we held spring training in Cairo, Illinois. There was a lot of rationing. Sugar rationing. Gas rationing, but ballplayers always had friends. We could get ration tickets.

I didn't get to serve. I was living in Abbeville, South Carolina, where my induction board was. Colonel Richie, the head of the camp in Fort Jackson in Columbia wanted to put together a baseball team. I was sent up there on a bus with the other inductees.

I got off the bus, and the MP who greeted me was [Dodger pitcher] Kirby Higbe. He was wearing his MP outfit, and he took me to see the colonel, and boy, was he wining and dining me.

I went through the physicals, and they saw I had broken my leg when I was a kid, so my right leg was wired together, and I had had forty stitches, and they had to rebreak it.

"Marty," said this major from Detroit, "If they want you to play baseball, that's fine. But I don't think you can march and do the things in the army a person has to do. I'm going to put you in 4-F."

I went back home, and a month later they called me back to Fort Jackson. Colonel Richie really wanted me on his team. I stepped off the bus, and there was Kirby again. He took me for another physical, and this major said, "What are you doing back here? I put you in 4-F."

"I don't know," I said. "They brought me back."

"I'm putting you in 4-F," he said.

This was right before the start of spring training. They called me a third time, but my draft board got mad, and they said, "No, we're not going to send you up again. You go to spring training, and if the war gets worse where we have to take 4-F into the army, you'll have to go."

I went to spring training in '43, and that was the end of it. We went to Cairo, Illinois, and we played in a little cow pasture and stayed in a teeny hotel there. The weather wasn't bad, and we spent half the time in a gymnasium throwing the ball around. The St. Louis Browns trained at Cape Girardeau, right up the road.

We started riding on day coaches. It didn't bother anyone. We were young, and we coped. We went on and played the games feeling we were helping out the morale of the country. We were offering a kind of service, we felt, though we weren't in the army. We were doing something to keep baseball alive.

Very few Cardinal players went to the war. Johnny Grodzicki, a good ol' Polish boy, was one of the Cardinals' best prospects. Johnny was a paratrooper, and he came back with a bad leg. He tried to pitch, and he hung around for a few years hoping he'd come back, but he never did. Johnny Beazley was in the army, and the Cardinals played his army team in an exhibition game. Johnny hurt his arm pitching against us. He babied it for a couple of years, but it never came back.

We ran away with the pennant in 1943. [The Cardinals won 105 games.] If you had your choice, you would lead from the first day until the end of the season. But it was more exciting in '42, when we came from behind and won it. That year, Stan Musial became a star. [In 1943, Musial had 220 hits and batted .357. He was also MVP in 1946 and 1948.] If you don't like Stan Musial, you don't like nobody. Stan was a natural. I can remember when the 1942 World Series was over in New York, he didn't come back to St. Louis to celebrate. He was going home to Donora, Pennsylvania. Stan was saying good-bye to everyone and crying like a baby. He had a good heart.

But Stan was just a good ol' country boy. We had a lot of good ol' country boys on our team. It didn't take long for Stan to become famous. He curled up like a corkscrew, and his stance was the talk of anyone who looked at him.

"He can't hit like that," everyone said, and the whole time he was whacking the ball all over the place. If you don't like Stan, you don't like anybody.

Stan loved hitting in Ebbets Field. He just had confidence against the Dodger pitchers. One day, he hit four home runs in Brooklyn, and the next day there was a cartoon in the paper with all those balls going out of the park. [Musial hit .550 in Brooklyn.]

Stan wasn't a bad outfielder. He knew how to play. He could run, though he had a bad arm. He was a good base runner, but he didn't steal a lot of bases. He didn't have to. He had good power. If you ever saw Stan undressed, he had a lot of muscles in his shoulders. One time I asked him, "How does the ball look to you?"

To me, it looked like an aspirin tablet.

"Looks like a grapefruit," he said to me.

And he wasn't lying. He had good eyes.

I never saw Stan mad. He was always kidding with everybody. He liked to tell jokes and play the damn harmonica. He was a very popular man.

In '43, we played the Yankees again in the World Series, but this time we didn't have the intensity, didn't have the feeling, didn't have the desire to win like we did in '42. It was a war year, and I don't think our minds were on it. That's a poor excuse because they beat us. But we didn't have the same feeling. Our minds were on something else.

In 1944, we scared 'em. [The Cardinals began the '44 season with a 45–15 record.] We again won the pennant, and we played the Browns in the World Series. Because of the war, the competition wasn't as good, but I don't ever remember playing a game where I said, "I wish we had so and so." No. We just played the game. The war was never mentioned.

I was named the Most Valuable Player in 1944, but it didn't mean a thing to me. It did when I got to be fifty years old. I found I had won when I was in Atlanta, visiting my wife's mother. Someone called me and told me I had won the Most Valuable Player Award, but I wasn't impressed. I didn't even know what the hell it was. I didn't think about things like that too much. Now, after years have passed, I feel, hey, that's pretty nice.

The Cardinal players and the Browns players didn't know each other much because they were on the road when we were home, and we were on the road when they were home. The only time we met them was when we played them in an exhibition game. In 1944, they had a good ball club.

Everybody in St. Louis loved the Browns, but they went to see the Cardinals play. The Cardinals were a better, more famous ball club, though the Browns were here first. Nobody went to see the Browns, except that year. When they started winning, they picked up support. Though we didn't draw much either.

The Browns owned Sportsman's Park. We were their renters. During the last week of the '44 season we paid a lot of attention to whether they were going to beat the Yankees for the pennant. We didn't have any special feeling for them. When we ended up in the World Series together, we knew we could beat them.

We felt the Browns were nothing, but after we played them the first game and Denny Galehouse beat us [2–1], we changed our minds. They had a pretty good ball club, and we were lucky to beat them. During that whole series, you couldn't see the baseball in that ballpark. There was a lot of sunshine, and the people sitting in the center field bleachers all were wearing white shirts. I never saw such a background. It was horrible. You could hardly see the ball. The pitching wasn't that good, but the hitting was horrible. We couldn't see the damn ball. [In six games, the Cardinals scored sixteen runs and the Browns twelve.]

I didn't tell anybody, but I had the flu during the series. I had a temperature of 102 and 103 the whole series, and I was sick as a dog. My wife was pregnant with our second child, and she had gone home, and I was staying at the Melbourne Hotel. As soon as the game was over, I drove over and got in bed, and for three days all I had was orange juice. I was weak as hell.

I played all right. I didn't do great. We won 4–2.

We should have won the pennant in '45. The Cubs did. We had a better ball club than they did. I can't tell you why we didn't win. We didn't have the zip and desire.

In 1946, Eddie Dyer became our manager when Breadon wouldn't pay Bill Southworth what he wanted. At the start of the season, Breadon sold Walker Cooper to the Giants for $175,000. He had traded Mort the year before to the Braves. It goes back to the minor leagues when Walker and Dyer didn't get along. Walker never did like Dyer. Dyer admitted that they had had words in the minors, but he swore he never did anything to Walker that would hurt him personally. But getting $175,000 for Walker Cooper back then was important money. Nobody asked me. 'Cause Walker was one of the mainstays of our team. I never talked to Mr. Breadon about it. I don't have any inside dope on what he thought.

Despite our success, we were paid small salaries. Everybody knew the Cardinals were a cheap ball club. We didn't know what guys on other teams were making. Back in those days, it was an honor to be in the big leagues, and we didn't want to do anything to rock the boat. The players would talk about Mr. Rickey and Mr. Breadon being cheap as part of our conversation. We didn't see much of their money, but if you argued too much, you risked going back to Rochester.

Then in '46 three of our players—Max Lanier, Lou Klein, and Freddy Martin—went to Mexico to play. Max Lanier started the season 6–0. He was making $6,000, and the Pasqual brothers offered him a $20,000 bonus and a three-year contract, and in the middle of the night they left for Mexico.

Stan Musial told me that the Pasqual brothers put $100,000 in cash in a suitcase and told him the money was his if he played in their league. He turned it down. I never had the good fortune to turn down $100,000. Pasqual never contacted me. And yet the smartest thing Stan did was turn them down. There was no guarantee the league was going to last, and it didn't, and all the players who went to the Mexican League were banned from major league baseball for five years.

After they left, guys were upset about them leaving, but not too long after we didn't discuss it much. It didn't seem to bother us. Even with a rookie manager [Eddie Dyer], we won the pennant again. Dyer was more or less like Southworth. He tried to keep you happy. I always liked Dyer, and he always liked me.

The Cards and the Dodgers finished the 1946 season even, and we played them two out of three. They flipped a coin, and Leo Durocher won and chose to play the first game in St. Louis so he could play two in Brooklyn. Leo was a gambler, and he took the best odds. But you have to travel, and we won the first two games, and he never got to play that third one.

During that first game Leo was standing on third base. He noticed how skinny our infielders were.

"Kurowski, Marion, Schoendienst, Musial, you couldn't get a pint of blood out of your whole infield," he said.

I used to argue with old Leo all the time. He was fun. He was a showman. His wife was Laraine Day, a movie star. He was in the Gashouse Gang. They tell me Leo was a pretty good ballplayer.

"Come on, Leo," I'd say. "Do something."

Howie Polett, my roommate, won twenty games for the Cards in '46, and he won the first playoff game 4–2. Two days later, Murray Dickson won. Joe Garagiola was the hitting star. Joe was a lot better ballplayer than he credits himself.

We played the Boston Red Sox in the World Series, and we used the Boudreau shift against Ted Williams. I stayed at shortstop. Our third baseman, Whitey Kurowski, moved over to the right side along with Red Schoendienst and Stan. Ted never did try to hit the ball my way. [Ted, injured, hit .200 with only one RBI.]

The All-Star Game was played at Fenway Park that year, and the American League beat us 12–0. Ted hit two home runs. I was playing shortstop, and as Ted was coming around second base he gave me a wink, and he said, "Kid, don't you wish you could hit like that?"

Ted was an ornery devil. You know the trot he had? He was bouncing around, and he said, "Don't you wish you could hit like that?"

I was speechless. I just looked at him as he went on by.

The Red Sox were leading in the World Series three games to two. Harry Brecheen pitched a shutout to tie it at 3–3, and in the eighth inning of Game 7 Enos Slaughter made his famous run from first base on a single to score the winning run.

I was the next hitter on deck, so I saw the whole play. Harry [Walker] hit the ball into short left-center field, and Leon Culberson was out there, and he got the ball in to Johnny Pesky. Pesky was out on the edge of the grass, and I could see right quick that Pesky didn't have a chance to throw Enos out.

Mike Gonzalez was our third base coach. He was from Cuba, and he had an accent, and Mike was hollering, "No, no, no," and Enos said, "I thought he was saying go, go, go."

And it was no contest. In defense of Pesky, no one told him where to throw the ball. His back was to the infield, and nobody was telling him what to do, which is a sin. The second baseman should have been hollering, "Home, home, home."

That little hesitation—Pesky dropped his arm and turned around to throw, and he had to double pump, and it was no contest. And Pesky didn't have the greatest arm anyway. So I can't blame Pesky for that at all. Whenever I'd see Harry, I'd say, "No one ever says you're the one who hit the ball." Harry didn't get any credit at all. It really wasn't that exciting a play. I didn't even have to tell Enos to slide, even though he slid across home plate.

Later, Enos told me, "I was going all the way."

In 1947, Jackie Robinson came up to the Dodgers. First of all, it was no surprise. He played at Montreal for a year, and everybody knew he was coming to the big leagues because he was that kind of ballplayer. It was the press that made such a big deal of it. And they kept talking about the Cardinals going on strike.

I never heard of such a thing in my life. Nobody in their right mind would do such a thing. They said we hated Jackie. We didn't hate Jackie any worse than we hated anyone else on the Brooklyn ball club—and we hated the Brooklyn ball club.

There were so many stories. Reporters would call me, and I'd tell them, "I was there, and I didn't see anything you guys are talking about."

Striking? We thought that was ridiculous. Sure, we didn't like Jackie Robinson. We didn't like anybody on the Dodgers. But that had *nothing* to do with Jackie Robinson being black.

One time, Enos stepped on him at first base. I don't think Enos did anything. I don't remember anyone doing anything that they wouldn't have done against a white person. Just because he was black, they made a big deal out of it. Did Enos say he did anything wrong? I never heard Enos say anything he did wrong.

I can't think of anything in baseball that has so many false remarks than the Jackie Robinson story. I never saw one Cardinal player—sure, Terry

Jackie Robinson. National Baseball Hall of Fame

Moore and Harry Walker didn't like him. They didn't like anybody. It had nothing to do with his being black. The press made it seem it was because he was black, but that wasn't the case at all. By the way, Jackie Robinson was a fierce competitor, too. He would step on you if you got in the way.

So many of these stories are false. But he got a lot of publicity, and he packed them into the ballparks. When he got into the league, you could hardly get in the ballpark for the blacks showing up. You know blacks don't go to ball games today. They don't support the club. Not at all. But they sure came to Sportsman's Park to see Jackie. You never saw so many black people in your life. Jackie Robinson drew them in. He sure did.

Another reason whites resented him: black players were going to take their jobs. The players had a perfect setup, a white fraternity. A lot of blacks could have played major league ball.

Jackie was a challenge to play against. He hit the ball hard. When he hit a ground ball to you, it was hit hard. One time, I picked him off. I had the honor of picking off the famous Jackie Robinson at second base. He didn't argue. He just dusted himself off and walked off like everybody else does. But he was aggravating. He was always jumping up and down. He got on your nerves.

I managed Satchel Paige. Oh Lord. Oh yes. And you can have Satchel. You know why? He ran the club. Not me. Everything Satchel wanted, Bill Veeck would do. Veeck loved Satchel.

One time, I fined Satchel $5,000. What did he do? He almost got us killed. I was managing the St. Louis Browns, and we were playing an exhibition game in Providence, Rhode Island. The Browns were fading. We didn't have enough baseballs to take batting practice. Bill was trying to get money wherever he could, and so played Providence on our way from New York to Boston on an off day.

We had a good crowd, a sellout. Must have been 15,000 people there. The sportswriters started coming down from the press box wanting to know, "Where is Satchel?"

I didn't know he wasn't there. The Browns had advertised that he was going to pitch.

"If you find him," I said, "I'll pitch him."

Satchel had skipped the game. Bill Durney, our traveling secretary, said to me, "The fans want their money back. They are ready to lynch us."

"Bill," I said, "get the money, and you get out of here."

It was a bad situation. They wanted to see Satchel pitch.

The next morning, we took the train to Boston. I walked into the Kenmore Hotel, and there was ol' Satchel sitting there in the lobby.

"Satchel," I said, "you almost got us lynched last night."

"What did I do?" he asked.

"You were supposed to pitch last night, and everyone wanted to see you pitch, and they wanted their money back," I said. "That's going to cost you $5,000. I'm calling Veeck right now."

Satchel didn't have an excuse. He wasn't sick.

"Hell, Veeck isn't going to take his money," Durney said.

One day, when I was managing we had a clubhouse meeting, and Sugar Cain, one of our pitchers, asked me, "Marty, why is it you make all us white boys do all these things, but you never make Satchel run?"

"You got me there, Sugar," I said. "But number one, Satchel can't run. And number two, when you get to be sixty-five years old, you can do that."

Satchel wouldn't do anything, and you couldn't tell him anything. He'd sit in that big rocking chair down in the bullpen. Oh, he was a character.

Satchel was a bad guy to have on a club. He'd keep everyone on the club up all night. He was telling all his stories, and everyone was listening.

A few years later, I was managing the White Sox, and Bill Veeck called me.

"Marty," he said, "if I get you Satchel, you can win a pennant."

"Veeck," I said, "no way am I going to manage Satchel again."

I liked listening to him, too. He could tell all his funny stories, and when he'd get to bathing, taking a shower, he was a pretty black person. He'd take his talcum powder and put it all over him, and he'd be as white as me when he got through. Then he'd rub snake oil on him. He'd rub his arm with it.

He was good copy, but he was bad for the manager. Satchel would no more pay attention to me than the man in the moon.

· *4* ·

Rex Barney

The last game I pitched I got beat, and Leo said to me, "You will never pitch for me again as long as you live. I don't care if Mr. Rickey loves you. You're finished with me. I'm going to send you so far an air mail stamp won't find you."

—Rex Barney

*R*ex Barney was one of baseball's first phenoms. He pitched for the Brooklyn Dodgers in 1943 at the age of eighteen. His record was 4–7 with a 2.88 ERA. He then enlisted in the army to fight in World War II, and after winning two Purple Hearts and a Bronze Star, he returned to the Dodgers in 1946. He struggled with wildness in 1946 and 1947, but in 1948 he put it all together, winning fifteen games while striking out 138 batters, second in the league. That year, he pitched a no-hitter against the New York Giants. He had thrown a one-hitter against Philadelphia the year before. He was that good. Barney had a ringside seat to comment on the managerial skill of Leo Durocher and to watch the entrance of Jackie Robinson into the major leagues.

Rex Barney. National Baseball Hall of Fame

Injuries and his inability to control his pitches cut short his career, and he was out of the majors at the end of 1950.

Barney became the PA announcer for the Baltimore Orioles in 1974, and he was there until 1991. Barney died on August 12, 1997.

Rex Barney: I was born and raised in Omaha, Nebraska. I played high school baseball in April and May, even though the average temperature is twenty above zero, and I was on a world championship American Legion team in 1939. I was a pitcher, and scouts followed me. I pitched the championship game against Kerwin, Illinois. We won 4–1, and I had seventeen strikeouts, setting a record.

At the time, I felt I was going to be a major league player, because that's all I ever wanted to be from the time I knew what it was all about. My mother told me the other little guys in the neighborhood would play cops and robbers or cowboys and Indians, while mine was always baseball, basketball, or football. As long as I could get onto a team, that's what I wanted to do. I went to a Jesuit high school, and I was a better basketball player. They didn't have Little League, but they did have midget American Legion, and when I was eight, nine, and ten I was a catcher and an outfielder. I was a catcher because no one wanted to play there. Eventually, I was the tallest kid in the neighborhood, and the theory was that the tallest kid could throw the hardest, and in fact I did throw harder than anyone else, and so I became a pitcher.

I had thirty scholarship offers to play college basketball. Notre Dame was the biggest school. Also, schools throughout the Midwest: Purdue, Indiana, Nebraska, and Creighton. The war was coming, and I was eighteen, and if I chose a scholarship I knew I would be drafted right away, so I went to the draft board and said, "If I sign a professional baseball contract, would you let me finish the season and then go into the service?"

They said yes.

Every major league team was interested. I worked out with the Yankees, the Giants, Detroit, Philadelphia. Detroit was the most impressive because when I went to Detroit I was only a junior in high school. I was only seventeen years old. The Tigers had three kids working out: Bobby Brown, who played for the Yankees; Artie Houtteman, who pitched for Detroit; and me, three seventeen-year-olds who made it to the major leagues.

A priest at Jesuit tutored me so I could graduate a month before my class, and I signed with the Brooklyn Dodgers. Larry MacPhail owned the club at that time, but Mr. Rickey took over right at that time, and I was to get the biggest bonus in the history of baseball, which was $5,000.

But here's how I got the $5,000. They gave me $2,500 when I signed, and I was to get the other $2,500 if I came back from World War II in one piece and could still play. That's what I signed. That's Mr. Rickey.

I didn't argue. I used to think $2,500 was all the money in the world. Nobody else got any money. My father probably worked for twenty-five years for $2,500. To get $2,500 in one lump sum when you're eighteen years old and you're from Omaha, Nebraska—you're a millionaire. You've got it all.

But what was I going to do with it? My father and mother didn't have a lot of money, so I gave it to them. I made the great salary of $250 a month in Durham, North Carolina, for the month of May. I did very well there [4–6 with a 3.00 ERA], and they sent me to Montreal in the International League. I played a month in Montreal in '43, and in July they took me to the majors. And I'm sitting in the dugout with Dixie Walker, Billy Herman, Augie Galan, Arky Vaughn, Mickey Owen, Kirby Higbe, and Whitlow Wyatt, people who three months before I'd ask them for their autograph.

Three months before that I was in high school. When I was sent to Montreal, I was sent with another pitcher by the name of Hal Gregg. We both were then sent to Brooklyn, the first time I had ever been to New York City in my life. It was the first time I had ever been to a major league ballpark. I was so scared I wanted to go back to Omaha. All my life I wanted to be a major league ballplayer, and here I wanted to quit.

Hal Gregg and I went to Mr. Rickey's office. It was 10 or 11 in the morning. Mr. Rickey said to me, "You're not going to really pitch. We know you're going into the service as soon as the season is over. If we're behind 14 or 15 runs, we might let you pitch an inning or so, but we feel you're a major league ballplayer, and when you get out of the service, that's what we want you to be. We want you to get acquainted with what it's like."

Which was fine with me. The Dodgers were paying me the grand sum of $500 a month when nobody else was making any money.

I went to the ballpark. We were playing at 1:30 that afternoon, a doubleheader against the Chicago Cubs. Our manager, Leo Durocher, came up to me, and he said, "Kid, when did you last pitch?"

"Four days ago," I said.

"You're going to start the second game of today's doubleheader."

Hell, I'd have gone back to Omaha in a flash. I didn't want any part of that. Here I was, two months out of high school, and I'm pitching in a major league ballpark.

The first major league game I ever saw, I pitched in. I didn't know what was going on, but the first pitch I threw in the major league was against Eddie Stanky, and I hit him right in the middle of the back.

I left in the seventh with a 2–2 tie game. And four days later, I came back and won my first major league game against the Pittsburgh Pirates. Years later, when the war was over and I was back with the Dodgers, Stanky was with the Dodgers. Durocher was the manager and he was taking me around the clubhouse, and he introduced me to Stanky, and Stanky said, "I remember the son of a bitch. He hit me right in the middle of the back, his first pitch in the major leagues."

I finished the '43 season on a Sunday in September [2–2 with a 6.35 ERA], and on Monday I was in the army. That's how quick it happened. Then I went overseas.

In '46, I was still overseas during spring training. I joined the club on opening day. The second day of the season, Ed Head pitched a no–hit, no–run game. In '46, Jackie Robinson was with Montreal, our Triple-A team, and the Dodgers determined we should go to spring training in '47 in Havana, Cuba, because of Jackie. Mr. Rickey didn't want a black playing in the South, not in Florida or anywhere else. He didn't want a black exposed to that.

We stayed at the Nacional Hotel. Montreal came to train with us, and they stayed at a military school outside of Havana. We had someone to play every day. The Cuban teams didn't match up to how we played. Jackie was with Montreal until opening day.

We then toured through the South, and we finished our '47 exhibition season with a three-game series against the Giants. Jackie didn't play. He was still with Montreal.

Monday was a day off, and he joined us, and on Tuesday Brooklyn opened the season. When Jackie first came into the clubhouse, I was the first player on the Dodgers to walk up to him, and I wished him luck.

"I hope you can help us," I said to Jackie, "because we need you." .

I was the opening-day pitcher. We had an old redneck clubhouse man, and instead of a locker, he had Jackie hang his uniform on a nail for a couple of months. He wouldn't even give him a locker.

When we were in Panama some of the Dodgers plotted against Jackie. We all knew about it. Jackie knew about it. The front office people stopped it.

That first season that Jackie was with us, we went to Pittsburgh, Chicago, St. Louis, the first trip around the league with Jackie, and a lot of players on other teams wanted to strike. They didn't even want to go on the field. In those days, 90 percent of the baseball players came from the South. Now they come from the West, California and Arizona. But there were a lot of redneck people. They would look at you and say, "My ancestors, my kinfolk, they'd kill me if they found out I was playing with a black man." And they didn't say "black man," but it's the only kind of talk I can use. That's the way they were.

It was ridiculous. The first time we played the Cardinals, Jackie was play-ing first, and Enos Slaughter was up, and Slaughter grounds out by ten feet, and he stepped almost on Jackie's thigh, kind of jumped on it. And Jackie went down. He was very upset.

Slaughter thought he was doing the right thing. The next inning Jackie got a hit, and he was standing on first, and Stan Musial was the first baseman.

"I don't care what happens," Jackie said to Stan, "when I get to second base, I'm going to knock someone into center field. I don't care what kind of play it is, he's going down."

Jackie Robinson. National Baseball Hall of Fame

Stan, being the gentleman he is, said, "I don't blame you. You have every right to do that."

Jackie told us later it took all the anger out of him. He didn't have the heart to do it after that. Because Musial was such a class guy. Stan understood. His teammate did it, but still he understood human feelings, and I guess Stan being Polish could appreciate what was going on, and he didn't like it. Stan never played that way. Stan was a magnificent ballplayer all his life and he was a gentleman.

We were going to go back to Havana in '48, but Mr. Rickey met with Trujillo, the dictator of the Dominican Republic, and he evidently gave us a better money deal. That was the first spring training when Jackie was with a major league club, and we were down there for three months in this magnificent hotel, and it was really great.

We played exhibition games in Panama at the Panama Canal. We played in Puerto Rico, in Nicaragua, and in Venezuela. You can imagine how much fun that was. It was almost like the navy. Join the Dodgers and see the world. And we had Jackie to thank.

When we returned to the United States, we toured the South. Everything was set by then. We were the first white team ever to play with a black player in places like Macon, Georgia; Columbus, Georgia; Atlanta; and in South Carolina. We got threatening letters they were going to kill Jackie. Jackie was scared to death.

The first town and the worst we played in was Macon. Mr. Rickey had brought in Sam Lacy, the sports editor of the *Baltimore African-American*, special so Jackie would have someone to room with. At every city we went to, including major league cities, Jackie would be met at our train by the local black doctor, lawyer, or best businessman to take him to his home. Because Jackie wasn't allowed to stay with us at the hotels.

The first time we played at Macon, it was sold out. Jackie Robinson was going to play. They roped off the field. It was unbelievable. And just as our bus got there from the hotel, Jackie and Sam Lacy pulled up in a car. We were going in the entrance when we were met by this big policeman. A sign said, Entrance for Whites Only. We started going in, and Jackie started going in, and I was behind him, when this big policeman said, "You can't come in here. Can't you read this sign?"

Jackie got petrified.

"He can't go in this entrance?" our manager, Leo Durocher, said.

"No, he can't."

"Then we're not going in," Leo said. "You know what that means?"

Now the policeman got scared to death, because it was the biggest crowd in history, so he let us all in. It was the first time a black man had ever played with white ballplayers in the South. We were on the field, Jackie and Pee Wee standing together, and Bruce Edwards and I were having a catch, and I can remember Pee Wee saying, "Jack, how about you going and standing next to Rex?"

"Why?" Jackie asked.

"Because if they shoot at you and miss, I don't want them to get me," Pee Wee said.

Well, that took the edge off.

The greatest person Jackie ever had wasn't Mr. Rickey, and it wasn't me. It wasn't anybody but Pee Wee Reese. Because Pee Wee was from Louisville, Kentucky, and he was as southern as anyone on the club. A lot of southerners asked to be traded. Dixie Walker and Bobby Bragan wanted to be traded. They didn't want to be seen on the field with a black player because of their background. It didn't matter to me. In Nebraska, I had played against blacks all my life. I didn't know any difference.

I used to say to Pee Wee, "I don't understand your thinking. All these other southerners . . ."

Pee Wee said, "Rex, we have a great club. We always come *this close.* With this guy, we can win. Without him, we may not win. It's pure and simple. I told Jackie that. I'm telling you, together we can win this."

Pee Wee did something—the first time it ever happened I was pitching. I was warming up and I could hear Ben Chapman, the manager of the Phillies, was the most antiblack manager I've ever known. In those days, managers coached third base. I have to use this language because I have to quote him. Chapman said, "Jackie, you nigger son of a bitch, you shoeshine boy," and while the Phillies were warming up, Chapman said to Pee Wee, "How can a southerner like you play with that nigger bastard."

Pee Wee Reese and Jackie Robinson. Author collection

We were in Philadelphia, and with Jackie standing on first base, Pee Wee walked over and put his arm around him, and he was saying, *This is my boy. This is the guy we're going to win with.*

Well, it drove Chapman right through the ceiling. That's why Pee Wee was the most instrumental person for Jackie Robinson to be a success, except for Jackie himself and his wife, Rachel. But Pee Wee more than anybody because Pee Wee was from the Deep South. Pee Wee understood things a little better than most, and still does. Pee Wee was a great Robinson admirer. They became very close friends. But not for that reason. They understood each other. [Note: Other Dodger players told me Pee Wee did the same thing in Cincinnati and in Boston as well as in Philadelphia. I wrote a children's book titled *Teammates* about Pee Wee and Jackie's relationship.]

From the time we got Jackie, we started winning. In '47, Jackie played first base, and then he moved to second base after Eddie Stanky was traded. Stanky was one of the players raised in the South, and he didn't want to play with Jackie, and Mr. Rickey traded him right away. Mr. Rickey traded people right away if they didn't want to be with Jackie. Kirby Higbe was gone. Dixie Walker, too. Quick. He went to Pittsburgh.

We traded Dixie Walker, Kirby Higbe, Gene Mauch, Cal McLish, and other players to the Pittsburgh Pirates for Preacher Roe, who was a nothing pitcher at the time, and Billy Cox, a mediocre infielder. It was a tremendous gamble on Rickey's part. He was hung in effigy all over Brooklyn. Dixie Walker was the "People's Cherce" and Mr. Rickey was nothing. For some fans, that was it. They would never go to the ballpark again.

Well, look up what happened from '47 on. We won pennant after pennant after pennant with the likes of Preacher Roe and Billy Cox.

Mr. Rickey was right.

For Jackie, his first couple of years were horrendous. You and I couldn't have done it. You couldn't do it and survive. If people had called me those kind of names, I couldn't have survived. Some of it came from his own teammates—to his face. Hey, he was playing on hallowed ground. You're not allowed to do that.

A lot of us saw this and we couldn't understand it. I still don't understand it. But the opposition to Jackie was horrendous. What he had to listen to was horrendous. But for two years he put up with it.

Then we went to the Dominican Republic for spring training. We had a little get-together in the clubhouse among the guys who had been there a long time.

"I realize there are some people here who don't like me," Jackie said at the meeting. "A lot of players in the league knock me down, spike me, did all these things to me, and I put up with it.

"I am convinced I am a major league ballplayer. That's what I'm here for. To play baseball. And from this point on, I will take nothing from no one on this team or any other team—umpires or anybody else."

And from that point on, Jackie asserted himself. In 1949, Jackie took over, and from '49 on he was what he wanted to be. He was the most exciting player I had ever seen. Not the best, but the most exciting. If you had a chance to win in any way and you put him up there, you had a chance. A definite chance. Jackie was the most exciting player by far. I never saw anyone like him.

We'd go to other ballparks and pack the house. Having a black player, people came to see if he was a freak, to boo him or to cheer him, whatever, but the second he got on base, you could feel the whole ballpark was on the edge of their seats. Because they knew he was going to do *something*. It was just a matter of time.

Jackie played baseball with such abandon. Jackie was going to do something. Steal a base. He's the only player I've ever seen if he was the runner on first, and a sacrifice bunt was in order, he didn't go to second and stop. He kept going to third. On a bunt.

It got to where on a sacrifice bunt and he was on first, the third baseman would pick it up, and instead of throwing it, he'd stand there and hold it to stop him from going to third. He would get such a big lead that if they threw to first, he'd go to second.

He was not fast. He . . . was . . . not . . . fast, but he was quick. Jackie's first fifteen or twenty feet was the quickest you've ever seen. If you *tried* to pick him off first, he'd go to second. I've seen him hit the ball to right field, and if the right fielder bluffed a throw to first, he'd go to second. He was that quick.

And when he played, the ballparks came alive. Because they knew he was going to do *something*. It was sad he didn't get to the major leagues until he was twenty-eight.

Leo Durocher was the Dodger manager, and he could be terrible. Very tough. But I had played for a high school coach almost like him, and I found out when Leo yelled and screamed, he liked you and was trying to help you. He got on the people who played best for him, like Furillo, Pee Wee, myself, Stanky, Ralph Branca, and Hodges—when he yelled and screamed at you, you were all right. When he gave you the silent treatment, you were in a bunch of trouble. He threw shoes at me. He threw a chair. I was pitching at the Polo Grounds, and I had won five games in a row. This was in 1948. This was just before Leo went over to manage the Giants. I was his best pitcher. I was pitching every fourth day.

Leo was such a perfectionist. I was ahead 4–0 late in the game. We had gone over the hitters before the game, and he said, "Make Walker Cooper hit a fastball. As hard as you throw, he'll never be able to hit it."

Well, I got smart, and I threw him a curveball, and Cooper hit it in the seats. I eventually won the game 4–1, but Leo was so mad at me for throwing a pitch he told me not to throw that he threw a chair at me. And he was dead right.

I was pitching in another game, and there was a little slow roller to first base, and I was slow covering first base, and the runner was safe, and a run scored, and eventually it was the winning run. I lost 2–1. People had to grab Leo, he was so mad. He couldn't accept those mental errors. And he was right. I pitched a hell of a game, but I lost because of my mental error.

I don't think there will ever be another Durocher. I thought Leo was one of the best managers in all of baseball, not that he was much loved, but if you were having salary problems and I asked for *X* amount of dollars and Mr. Rickey would say, "No, we're not going to give it to you," I would go to Leo. I'm using *I*, but this goes for other players.

I'd say, "Leo, I want this amount of dollars, and he won't give it to me."

"I think you deserve it," Leo would say to you. "I'll get it for you." Or "I don't think you deserve *X*, you deserve this." And you'd take it. If he said he'd get it for you, he'd get it. He did that for me on two occasions.

I had won two games and lost five in late June of 1948, a terrible year. The last game I pitched I got beat, and Leo said to me, "You will never pitch for me again as long as you live. I don't care if Mr. Rickey loves you. You're finished with me. I'm going to send you so far an air mail stamp won't find you. I don't want anything to do with you. I'll never talk to you again. We're finished."

I was rooming with Ralph Branca at the time. Ralph kept saying, "Forget about it."

"I can't forget this," I said. Because I had been the opening-day pitcher, and I was supposed to do everything correct.

Four days later, we're playing a doubleheader in Philadelphia on July 4. We had used up all our pitchers, and Leo came to me and said, "All right. I'm giving you one more chance. You're going to pitch the second game of this doubleheader. We'll see what happens."

Well, I pitched a two- or three-hitter and won 5–0. I pitched a magnificent game. Then I reeled off five or six in a row, and Leo left the club and went to the Giants.

Leo was that type of person. He did scare me. But the circumstances were such that he had to use me, and luckily I got it all together.

Burt Shotton took over as manager. I'm anti-Shotton. I just thought the game got by him. I didn't like the cute Old Man thing he did with no uniform. I didn't think he gave his coaches enough authority. He and I had some personal problems. Maybe because Ralph Branca and I were so young, and we roomed together, and we were having a lot of success, and Shotton didn't go with it. We had a lot of fun. You could do that with Leo. Leo was strict, but at the same time you could have fun with him.

If you pitched well, Leo acknowledged it, and even if you pitched badly, he'd let you know about it. Shotton was cold and indifferent, and maybe my personality needed that pat on the back or the kick in the ass. Shotton had no emotions, and with that ball club in Ebbets Field in Brooklyn with those fans, for me Shotton never fit.

I never thought Shotton fit the organization. He fit Mr. Rickey because they were cut from the same mold. Mr. Rickey and Leo never really fit, but they respected each other and loved each other, and they worked hard for each other. Mr. Rickey and Leo put together a good organization. They took an organization that was terrible and nailed it together.

In 1946, we were picked to finish last, and we wound up in the playoff with the Cardinals. Because we got it together. Leo and a lot of hard work. We had a lot of talent coming back from the service, and guys wanted to show him they could do the job. We had more talent than they thought we ever had.

Mr. Rickey's whole idea was to sign every player in the world. Let all those glamour guys go to every club in the world, but you sign everybody else. If you sign five hundred kids, you're going to come up with five ballplayers. The other club would handpick all these super people and give them money—Mr. Rickey didn't give anybody anything. He just signed everybody, shake them all out, and you're going to come up with a handful of players.

He signed players no one else wanted. He signed Ralph Branca, who was turned down by the Giants and the Yankees. He signed Maury Wills, who played eight or nine years in the minor leagues. Nobody wanted Pee Wee Reese. He was too small. Larry MacPhail took a shot at him. Pete Reiser originally was with the Cardinals, but the Cardinals had signed a bunch of young kids, so they released him, and the Dodgers picked him up. With the Dodgers, nobody got a nickel from anybody

I broke my leg the last day of the season in 1948. I was pitching against Robin Roberts, and I slid into second, and I broke it in two places. I was ahead in the game, and I actually walked off the field, and then I pitched the next half inning, but the pain became so bad I couldn't handle it. It was two cracks, which sometimes is worse than a break.

The next day, I went to the doctor, and I was in a cast from October almost through January. I went to Vero Beach early to run and walk in the sand and try to build up the leg.

In 1949, I won ten ball games, but from that point on, I never had the same motion. I never had it again. And I pitched three more years after that. I never got into the same flow, and in baseball rhythm is everything, especially for a pitcher.

DiMaggio and Musial say I threw harder than anybody, but I would have given all that up for proper direction. Control is where it's at. It was nice to have that reputation for speed. We played the Yankees in an exhibition in 1947, and the first time Tommy Henrich saw me, he said to Campanella, "This guy came down from some other league. Where is he from? There is no chance."

Campy told me the story, and that's good, but I'd rather have a different reputation. There were times in my life when I was having so many problems—I can admit it now—I thought of committing suicide. I thought the world was over. I was twenty-eight years old, and I was finished. I really don't know what keeps you together.

Mr. Rickey sent me to a psychiatrist. I went to two of them. I went to the Menninger Clinic in Topeka, Kansas. I would talk to them for an hour, and they would say, "Christ, you're saner than we are."

Mr. Rickey was the only genius in all of baseball. If a guy was having a problem, Mr. Rickey would go to any length to try to straighten out that problem. If a player was having trouble, he'd ask, "Are you having family problems? Are you having wife problems? Are you having children problems? Is it something off the field?"

He said to me, "We know you have more talent than anyone we have. Is something wrong? Is there something causing all this? What is it?"

The only knock I got, and I got this from psychiatrists, who said, "You're overbright, you're overintelligent, you're overarticulate for what you're doing," but then I would ask, "Why did I have so much success in such a short time? Why could I put it together at such a young age, and I can't put it together now?"

People to this day ask me, "Now that you know so much, what would you do to correct it?" Hell, if I knew that, I would have pitched ten more years in the big leagues.

I don't have any regrets. I was a major league ballplayer, which is all I ever wanted to be in my life. I had a lot of success, though I know more than anybody that I never lived up to my full potential. As we sit here and talk, I was awesome. I really was. I was scary. I didn't know it then. Why did I have that? I don't know.

Sandy Koufax and I became very good friends over the years. The first time I met him, Koufax said, "I wanted to meet you for so long. I used to go see you pitch when I was a little kid. I've heard all about you, and for years at spring training, people said to me, 'You have a Rex Barney fastball.' I always wanted to know what that was."

"You have control," I said to Sandy. "That's the whole difference."

Stan Musial

> You could hear them whispering, "Here comes that man again. Here comes that man again."
>
> —Stan Musial

$\int$tan the Man Musial was born on November 21, 1920. He spent twenty-two seasons starring for the St. Louis Cardinals. He had a lifetime batting average of .331, made 3,630 hits, hit 475 home runs, drove in 1,951 runs, and was named to twenty-four All-Star teams. Three times, in 1943, 1946, and 1948, Stan was named the National League's most valuable player. Seven times he was the National League batting champion. The Cardinals retired his number 6, and he was elected to the Hall of Fame. He was married to his high-school sweetheart, Lillian, for almost seventy-two years. Given the name Stan the Man by the Brooklyn sportswriters because he hit so well in Ebbets Field, Stan Musial was one of the least egotistical of baseball's superstars. I interviewed him in 1999. Musial died at age ninety-two on January 19, 2013.

Stan Musial. Photofest

Stan Musial: I was signed in 1938 by the Cardinals as a pitcher. Any time you have the best arm in high school, they always make you a pitcher, but I was a wild left-handed pitcher and I walked a lot of guys. I don't understand why the Cardinals didn't sign me as a hitter. I was a fantastic high school hitter, you know. Why someone didn't see me as a hitter was a surprise.

I'm from Donora, Pennsylvania, and grew up a fan of the Pittsburgh Pirates. In June, after I got out of high school in 1937, I was waiting to hear from the Cardinals, and I didn't hear from them. I had a friend who knew Pie Traynor, and he took me down to Pittsburgh, and I worked out with the Pirates a couple days. I was pitching batting practice, and then I got my notice from the Cardinals to report to their farm club in Williamston, West Virginia. Well, I had to tell Traynor what transpired, and he asked, "Did your dad sign your contract?"

I was seventeen.

"Yeah, my dad signed the contract," I said.

"That sort of makes it official," Traynor said. "But if you're ever out of a job, come back and see us."

I spent my first two seasons pitching at Williamson, North Carolina, Class D. [His record was 6–6 with a 6.14 ERA and 9–2 with a 4.30.] In 1940, I was a pitcher at Daytona Beach, Florida, another D league. [His record there was 18–5 with a 2.62 ERA.]

My manager was Dickey Kerr, who had pitched for the White Sox in the 1919 World Series. I never asked him about it because in those days I didn't know anything about that. Dickey put me in the outfield when I wasn't pitching. We talked a lot about baseball, and we got to be good friends.

I hurt my arm the last week of the season. I was playing the outfield because Dickey liked the way I hit, and I dove for a ball, and I landed on my shoulder. I tried to pitch one game after that, and my arm was sore. In those days, they didn't send you to a doctor to get an examination. I figured my arm would get better over the winter.

Dickie invited my wife and I to live with him. He told me not to worry about my injury because he felt I would end up in the major leagues as an outfielder. He was right, of course. As the years went on, I repaid him by buying him a house.

I became an outfielder full-time in 1941. We trained in Hollywood, Florida, and when I started warming up my arm was still sore. We had an exhibition game between us pitchers. Branch Rickey, our general manager, was there, as was the Cardinals manager, Billy Southworth, and during the game I hit a long drive. There wasn't a fence out there, and Mr. Rickey told me he stepped it off to see how far I hit it.

I was sent to Springfield, Missouri, Class C, and it was amazing that I was able to go from Class C to the majors in one year. I played two and a half months in Springfield, and I was hitting right off the bat. I was hitting [.379], hitting [26] home runs, driving in a lot of runs, and in midseason I was sent to Rochester, which was Triple A. Tony Kaufman was my manager, and during the couple of months I played there, I led the league. I was hitting over .300, [.326] and when the season ended, I came home. In mid-September, I got a wire from the Cardinals, telling me to report to St. Louis.

We had a doubleheader against the Boston Braves, and Billy Southworth put me in the lineup. I got a couple of hits, and we won the game, and I was hitting .400 [.426] the last couple of weeks with the Cardinals. I was a rookie, and they gave all the rookies a hard time. They wouldn't let you take extra batting practice, but I was hitting in every game, so I hit it off pretty good with the guys.

Billy gave me a lot of confidence by playing me often. He let me play. He put me in the lineup. I'll tell you what happened. After I came down to St. Pete in 1942 for spring training, everybody expected me to keep hitting like I did. Well, in Florida I never did hit good because in those days we didn't have a background. They had them palm trees. They were waving, and with my stance I couldn't pick up the ball very well. So I didn't have a good spring training, but when we got to St. Louis we played the Browns two out of three exhibition games, and the first day Billy said to me, "You're in the lineup. You're playing left field." And with the better background, I got a couple of hits that day. I started hitting again. Yes, Southworth gave me a lot of confidence. I'm glad they didn't judge me by my hitting in Florida.

In 1942, we started slowly, and by August we were about thirteen games behind the Brooklyn Dodgers. Then our club began to gel. We had a young veteran club. We had good speed, good defense, good pitching, and we won thirty-five of the last forty-two games to finally catch the Dodgers. One reason we were able to catch them was that in July their center fielder, Pete Reiser, crashed into the outfield wall in St. Louis face-first trying to catch a ball hit by Enos Slaughter. We gained a game on the Cardinals, and I don't remember if he played any more that year, but it was a pretty serious injury.

We went to Brooklyn, and we beat them two out of three, and then went to Philadelphia and had a tough series there, but we kept winning.

That '42 Cardinals club was a great club. As I said, Billy Southworth was our manager, and he handled us very well. Everybody got along. Whitey Kurowski, Johnny Beazley, and I were rookies, and Marty Marion, Jimmy Brown, and Walker Cooper were veterans, so we had a young veteran club. Something about us, we gelled together. We spent a lot of time together. We went out and had dinner and we talked baseball. We had a good spirit among us. We had the Cardinals spirit that after a while we didn't think we could be beat by anybody. We were a *tough* club.

The 1942 season came down to the final day. We played the Cubs in a doubleheader at Sportsman's Park, and we had to win one of the two games. I know we won the first one because I caught the ball for the final out. Catching that last ball was a great thrill. We had worked so hard to come back from thirteen games out. We had to win almost every game at the end.

That Cardinals club in 1942 was one of the best clubs the Cardinals ever had. We had great pitching with Johnny Beazley, Mort Cooper, and Max Lanier, and we had good balance in our lineup with Hal Trosky and Walker Cooper from the right side and Slaughter and I from the left side.

We didn't have many characters on our team. Walker Cooper used to carry on. We went to New York, and a guy was sleeping in the lobby, and Walker gave him a hot foot. He also did it to the ballplayers. Our uniforms had belts, and Walker would put a lit cigarette in a player's belt. Other than that, we didn't have any oddballs.

We met the Yankees in the World Series in '42. They didn't faze us any, because we trained with the Yankees in St. Petersburg, and that spring we beat them three out of five games. They were a good club, a great club, but we knew them because we had played against them in the spring.

We lost the first game [7–4]. At first, we didn't do much against Red Ruffing, and then we rallied in the ninth. I came up with the bases loaded and two outs, and I hit a hard ground ball to first base, and that ended the game. But then in the second game, we came back. I drove in the winning run in the eight inning, and Enos Slaughter made a terrific play to throw a runner out at third, and then we went to New York, and we beat them three in a row. Ernie White and Max won games three and four, and Beazley won 4–2 in the finale.

It was quite a team. We were tough.

We went back to the World Series in 1943. We won the pennant by eighteen games. That year, I was voted the MVP for the first time, and it was because I moved from left field to right field. I'm left-handed, and in left field you're making awkward throws off balance. In right field, you're throwing naturally. I had had a year under my belt and, of course, this was during the war, so the caliber of baseball went down somewhat. A lot of guys left in '43. I had a good year. Oh yeah, I led the league in most everything. [He hit .357, had 220 hits, 48 doubles, 20 triples, and his slugging percentage was .562.]

I was a good fastball hitter and could get the bat on the ball. I had a feeling that nobody could throw the fastball by me. After they found I could hit the fastball, they started throwing me curves, and I could hit the curve. I always felt I could get the bat on the ball.

After we lost the World Series to the Yankees, during Christmas I went to Alaska to entertain the troops for the USO. Dixie Walker, Fritz Ostermuller of the Browns, myself, and another player visited some of the islands. We walked around and talked baseball with the soldiers.

Then in 1944, we met the Browns in the World Series. They won the American League pennant on the last day. We won 105 games and finished fourteen and a half games ahead of Pittsburgh, and were favored. Everyone thought we had a better club, but that was one of the toughest series because the Browns won the first game and we had to play catch-up. They played tough, and we had a hard time. They had Denny Galehouse. Nelson Potter had that screwball, and Sig Jakucki and Jack Kramer made up a pretty good pitching staff.

After we lost the first game, Blix Donnelly came in in relief in the eighth inning of Game 2 with the score tied. There were runners on first and second, and the Browns tried to bunt them over, and the batter laid down an almost perfect bunt, but Blix made a fantastic play and that got us out of trouble. He struck out seven, and we won in the eleventh. Jack Kramer beat us in Game 3, and we had to come back again. We were playing catch-up, and they played tough, and we had a hard time winning. I hit a home run in Game 4 that we won 5–1, and we won the last two games 2–0 and 3–1.

The funny thing about that World Series: the fans were rooting for the Browns. It kind of surprised me because we outdrew the Browns during the season. If you analyze the situation, the fans who were there were older men, and they loved the Browns during the good old days of George Sisler and Kenny Williams. They were old-time Brownie fans.

Then in 1945, I was drafted. We had a couple of children, and they started taking married men with children into the service. I went into the navy for fourteen months. I was there with a bunch of ballplayers. [He was assigned to Bainbridge Naval Training Center in Maryland.] The navy sent us to Hawaii, and all we did over there was play ball. We had an eight-team 14th Naval District League. I was in a ship repair unit. I was a cashier.

We played about four times a week. There were at least 100,000 men coming through Honolulu every day. Our stadium sat around 10,000, and all these sailors and army personnel would come to the games for relaxation and recreation.

Every team had big league players. Ted Williams and Billy Herman. Bob Scheffing. We even had an All-Star Game between the American and National Leagues. It was a good experience because we were able to play, unlike Bob Feller, who spent three years on an aircraft carrier. We could keep our hand in.

When I returned to the Cards in 1946, I was disappointed that Billy Southworth no longer was our manager. Eddie Dyer was manager. I didn't know Dyer. So many things were happening after the war. You're coming back. You're going to spring training. Southworth was going to the Boston Braves. I knew Lou Perini over in Boston was trying to build the Braves up, and he went after the best man available in Southworth. I don't know what happened between Billy and the Cardinals. He probably got such a terrific offer he couldn't turn it down. And the Braves did win the pennant in 1948. They had a great club, Spahn and Sain.

In '46, all the Cardinal veterans came back. Slaughter, Terry Moore, and I were in the outfield. They traded Johnny Mize to the Giants and made Dick Sisler the first baseman. They also traded Walker Cooper, upsetting the balance of our club, because Mize and Cooper were our right-handed power, and when we lost Cooper, the other teams started throwing a lot of left-handers, saving them for Slaughter and I, and that upset the balance. Joe Garagiola came in, and he was a left-handed hitter. Del Rice caught some, but we lost some power. Cooper was a power hitter.

We started slowly in '46. Dick Sisler was having problems. He had a great minor league record, but he had trouble hitting the high fastball, so Dyer asked me to take over at first base for a few games until Sisler got squared away. I stayed there for ten years. I didn't like first base. It was work. First base is work. But I stayed there ten years, believe it or not.

That year, we lost Max Lanier to Mexico. Max was 6–0 when he left. We also lost Freddie Martin, a good relief pitcher, and our second baseman, Lou Klein. They both went to the Mexican League, which was founded by the Pasqual brothers.

I got a call from Jorge Pasqual. He met me at my hotel room along with Mickey Owen, who he signed. They were trying to get me to go to Mexico. They laid five $10,000 cashier checks on my bed. Pasquale offered me $125,000 for five years. I was only making $13,500.

I told them I wasn't interested. I always wanted to be a big league ballplayer. No matter what they offered me, I told Mickey Owen, I wasn't going and don't bother me. Owen and Max, mostly Owen, kept calling me from Mexico City, and I told them I wasn't interested. I never had any desire to leave the Cardinals. Nah.

Our game has changed. It's strictly business now [1999]. Free agency has changed it. The players take the best offers. With the way baseball is structured today, the money is available, and it's the American system. You go where you can make the most money. You can't blame the ballplayers. But in those days, we didn't think about money as such. We enjoyed playing the game, loved baseball. Money was kind of secondary. I didn't think about anybody else but the Cardinals.

After we beat the Red Sox in the 1946 World Series, I went barnstorming with Bob Feller. We played Satchel Paige and his All-Stars. I played against

Stan Musial. National Baseball Hall of Fame

Paige and Jackie Robinson. I remember watching Robinson because he had signed with Brooklyn, and he was coming up the next year. I watched him hit. He had a short, choppy swing, and I watched him take infield. He wasn't graceful. One night, I told our players what I thought about him. I wouldn't have made a very good scout. I said I thought he might have some problems playing in the big leagues. Bob Feller had the same reservations. Jackie was a great competitor, but he wasn't graceful.

I played five or six games against those guys. I hit against Satchel Paige. I hit a line drive, walked a couple times, and got one hit off of him. Feller and I then went to Hawaii to play a couple games over there.

There were rumors the Cardinals were going to strike if Robinson played against us. We *never* had a meeting or talked about anything of that nature. We were coming East to play the Dodgers. Sam Breadon, who owned the Cardinals, was going to talk to our manager because we weren't going well, and from that conversation the stories came out that we might strike against the Dodgers and Robinson, but none of that was true. We never considered it. We never talked about it, never had any idea about it.

We had a lot of southern ballplayers on our club. I can't remember anyone saying anything about not playing. We never had a meeting or anything of that nature. There were rumors that Enos Slaughter and I had a fight over Robinson. I don't know how these stories came about. Enos always played hard. He was a battler. On that play where he spiked Robinson at first base in St. Louis—it was such a close play at first base, and Enos stepped on his foot. I don't know of any professional baseball player who would deliberately hurt another professional player. The same thing happened with Joe Garagiola. He tripped over Robinson at first base and Joe broke his shoulder.

We had our battles with the Dodgers. We were rivals. We knocked them down. They knocked us down. After the game was over, the next day we'd come out and do it again. It was part of the game.

After we won in '46, we finished second in '47, '48, and '49. We weren't far behind the Dodgers, but the Dodgers won because they brought up those three black ballplayers, Robinson, Roy Campanella, and Don Newcombe. They made the difference as far as winning the pennant. We weren't far behind them. We didn't sign a black player until 1955 when we signed Tommy Alston.

Just before Thanksgiving in '47, Breadon sold the team to Fred Saigh. Fred paid me my first decent salary. I was making $13,500 with Breadon in '46, and the next year Fred put a blank check in front of me and told me to sign it. I filled in $31,000.

Fred and I were pretty close. We were together for six years. He sold to Gussie Busch in '53. I had some good years in '49 and '50, and I won batting titles in '50, '51, and '52, and by then I was making $75,000 a year. Ted Williams was making $85,000, but I thought my salary was fair.

I came within one home run of winning the Triple Crown in 1948 [.378, 39 home runs, 131 runs batted in]. I had a home run that was rained out, and I had another ball I hit in Philadelphia in Shibe Park that hit the speakers above the fence. Frank Dascoli, the umpire, called it a two-base hit, and it should have been a home run. With one more home run, I would have led the league in everything.

Then in 1949, I was almost traded to the Pirates. I didn't know anything about it, but I heard the rumors. I didn't want to leave St. Louis.

Then in 1953, Fred Saigh sold the team to Gussie Busch. Gussie was trying to get a winner quickly, and he hired Frank Lane as his general manager, and Lane almost traded me away. Lane came in and started making trades. That was his reputation. He was "Trader" Lane. Lane traded Red Schoendienst. That was a big shock because Red was my roommate. I hated to lose Red. We were together ten years. Of course, that's when our club went downhill—any time you have too many front office changes. Our clubs in the 1950s didn't do well.

When I heard the rumors about being traded, I said I doubted I would go because I was in the restaurant business and doing well. In the end, Gussie had to choose between Lane and me, and he fired Lane, and Bing Devine took over, and that was the end of any talks of my being traded.

Then in 1958 I was holding out because I was making $60,000, and Ralph Kiner was making $90,000, and I told Bing, "I should be the highest-paid player in the National League. I'd settle for $91,000."

They called me in and I was told, "Busch decided to make you the first $100,000 player in the National League."

That was good news to me. Busch and I got along great. He was a great owner. He loved baseball. He'd come down to spring training and work out with us.

In 1959, Busch made Solly Hemus the manager. Solly was a younger manager. He didn't have any experience. Solly figured I was getting older, and he took me out of the lineup quite a bit. One time Busch called me out to Grant's Farm, and he asked me what I thought of Solly as a manager.

"I think Solly deserves a little more chance," I told him. *Maybe next year he'll let me play*, I thought, but I didn't play much the next year either, and it wasn't until Johnny Keane came in that he said, "Stan, you're my left fielder. You're going to play," so I got to play a little longer. And it was because of Johnny Keane that I got to set all those records. I passed Ruth in extra base hits. I was fourth in RBIs behind Cobb, Gehrig, and Ruth. It made a lot of difference.

We were playing in Milwaukee during the 1960 season, and I was standing outside the hotel when a limo pulled up, and out jumped Jack Kennedy, who introduced himself. He was making a speech at the hotel there.

"They tell me you're getting too old to play baseball," he said, "but they say I'm too young to be president. I think we will both do well."

That winter, his brother Ted called me and asked me if I would campaign for Jack, and I said, "I'd be glad to." We had a good group—Jeff Chandler, Whizzer White, James Michener, Arthur Schlesinger, Shelley Winters, and Angie Dickinson, and some of the Kennedy girls, and we campaigned in seven or eight states in Republican territory—Iowa, Idaho, Utah, Colorado. It was a week's trip, and that's where I got to know James Michener. We would pair off in the evenings and go have dinner.

I got very close to James Michener through the years. Michener once ran for Congress in Philadelphia, and he asked me to campaign for him, but I wasn't that interested in local politics. We kept in touch. We took trips together. Michener loved Eckert College in St. Pete, and in February we'd come down, and we'd have dinner once a week, and I got to know his wife, and we took a lot of cruises together. We were very close.

Michener loved baseball. He knew Robin Roberts very well, and one time I threw a party for him at this hotel [I was interviewing Stan at the Vinoy Hotel in St. Petersburg]. It was his seventy-sixth birthday, and I had Ted Williams here, Al Lopez, Robin Roberts.

During a game in Washington, DC, after he was elected president, Jack Kennedy called me up to his box, and I met his friends. He invited Mrs. Musial and I to the White House, and we had a nice visit. We knew Bob and Ethel Kennedy very well. My wife and I would go to McLean, Virginia, to visit them. I got to be very close to the Kennedys through the years.

I can remember coming to my restaurant around noon on the day Jack Kennedy was shot, and there was a newsflash. Everybody was . . .

The rest of my career was eventful. Through the years, I traveled with Bob Broeg, who wrote for the *St. Louis Post-Dispatch*, and he kept telling me, "I think you can get 3,000 hits." It kept me going until I finally got it. My idol, Paul Waner, had been the last player to reach 3,000 hits, and I broke his record in LA. I was number eight.

When I began my career in those days, you never thought about records. Or the Hall of Fame, which is the highest honor. I go up there every year. It's a great place to be. I enjoy going and meeting the new inductees.

I played a lot of years, enjoyed the game, had fun at it, and loved it. I particularly remember the fans in Brooklyn. They had great fans there. I didn't realize how well I hit in Ebbets Field until a fan sent me the stats of all the games I played there. It was unbelievable. I hit .525 one year. I played eleven games in Brooklyn and had twenty-three hits. The next year, I had twenty-four hits. No wonder those fans got excited when I started walking to the plate. You could hear them whispering, "Here comes that man again. Here comes that man again."

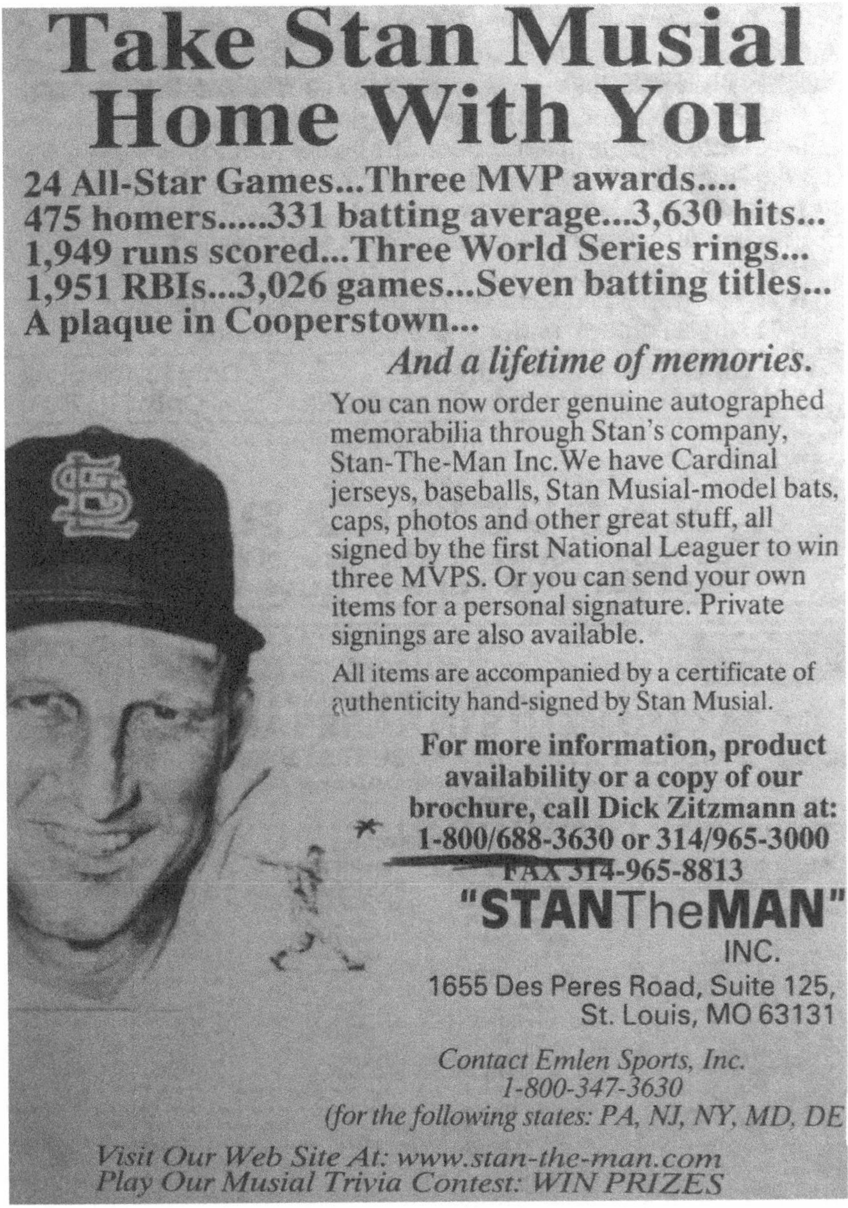

Stan Musial poster. Author collection

A couple writers picked up on that. I became Stan the Man. So I have a warm spot for Brooklyn fans. They gave me my nickname. They loved baseball. They backed their team. They were great. Brooklyn fans were special.

My last day in a Cardinal uniform was a happy moment and also a sad moment. I had played plenty of baseball. I was forty-two, and I was retiring. My time had come. I had played for St. Louis for all those years [1941–1963]. Those were great fans. And we got along with the writers and the press. They always sang my praises through the years, you know. They were instrumental in getting my statue put up there in St. Louis.

I enjoyed St. Louis.

· 6 ·

Tom Sturdivant

I wasn't a particularly heady pitcher. I was just an ordinary
pitcher who happened to be with a great ball club at the right
time.

—Tom Sturdivant

$\mathcal{T}$om Sturdivant was born on April 28, 1930. I interviewed him in the summer of 1974 at his home in Oklahoma City. Tom had starred for the New York Yankees in 1956 and 1957, winning sixteen games each year. He was the winner of the fourth game of the 1956 World Series, then was outshone in the next game when Don Larsen pitched his perfect game. Sturdivant injured his arm in 1958 and was traded to Kansas City. He played a bit part for Boston, Washington, Pittsburgh, Detroit, Kansas City again, and the New York Mets before he retired in 1964. His first love was always the Yankees. Sturdivant, a delightful, exuberant man, died on February 28, 2009.

Tom Sturdivant: I knew I was going to make the Yankees since I was six years old. Nobody else thought I was going to. I didn't have anything else to live for if I didn't make it.

I came up to the Yankees during spring training in 1955, and I pitched 35 scoreless innings in a row. Casey Stengel was our manager, and he called me over to the side, and he said, "Mr. Sturdivant, I see by the record two years ago your strikeouts were more than your innings pitched, and if you look at your record, you'll see your strikeouts were double your walks." He said, "What do you attribute this type of record?"

"Mr. Stengel," I said, "I attribute it to my fastball. It's my best pitch."

"Well son," he said, "when are you going to throw it?"

63

Tom Sturdivant. Author collection

Stengel knew I was a hard-headed competitive sort of an individual, and he just wanted me to throw a little harder, so I did. You can always throw a little bit faster.

Casey was a real great person at knowing what his personality could do. He knew how to treat ballplayers. Some people you have to build a fire under, and others you have to pamper and treat a different way. Some players, like Bob Turley, couldn't be chewed on. Stengel couldn't come out and say the same thing to him that he could to me. He'd say it to me, and I'd likely hit the next batter. Sometimes he'd call me a Dumb Dutchman. And he'd put a sumbitch on the end of it. Then the limpy, gimpy sawed-off son of a bitch would walk off, and I'd be so mad I'd want to kill him. He'd get me fired up. They might hit the ball nine miles, but they knew it had been thrown.

This is where Stengel was great. He knew how to treat each player.

It sure was funny: the sportswriters had a hard time understanding Mr. Stengel, but I never did. He never talked Stengelese to us. We always understood exactly what he meant.

Stengel was a very good baseball manager. Very few managers could have managed that Yankee ball club. I mean *managed* it. Stengel was a very good psychologist.

In my opinion, I think we had the best ball club in the world. We had a lot of stars. On another ball club, they would have been superstars in their own right. It's hard to have a Mantle and a Maris on the same ball club with a Berra and a Ford and a Skowron and a Howard. And Carey and Blanchard and a Richardson, a McDougald, and a Coleman. You know what I mean? And a Turley. And a Larsen and Kucks. And a Duren.

On a lot of ball clubs, you could name four or five players. On our club, you could name twenty players. And Casey kept them all in line. Ryne Duren was a tough person to manage. I wasn't the easiest person to manage, and Mantle was probably the easiest one. The superstars are easier to manage than the players who are really fighting for it.

And Mickey'd give you anything. He'd loan you money. He never asked you for it back. And I imagine a lot of people never paid him back. The theory was, if they weren't good enough to pay him back, then they wouldn't get any more. He was tremendous with rookies because he knew they were broke. He remembered when he came up he didn't have the money to bring his wife up here. It might take them a year or two to pay him back, but they were so grateful.

I imagine the pressure on Mantle was greater on him than it was on anybody because though the people came out to see the Yankees, they came to see Mantle. The Yankees didn't get booed. Mantle got booed. Why? Because Mantle was the greatest ballplayer walking. Why did they cheer the

Mickey Mantle. National Baseball Hall of Fame

Mets? They were the worst ballplayers in America. I played with the Mets. You'd walk out there, and man, they'd just cheer you. When I first went out there, they remembered me as a Yankee, and they gave me a booing ovation. And after I got killed, they gave me a standing ovation! They figured if I had enough guts to go out there with the junk I had left, I needed an ovation.

In 1955, my first year, the reporters kept saying the Yankees didn't have any pitching, but we kept winning with what we had. They were waiting for me to take charge and break loose, but I didn't pitch much. We had a pretty fair pitching staff. They had traded for Bob Turley and Don Larsen, and we had Whitey Ford and Johnny Kucks. All had low earned run averages, and all of them had real good stuff, and I felt very fortunate just to get there.

In 1956, I didn't get to pitch until three days before the trading deadline. We were getting ready to go on a road trip. It was a Sunday afternoon, and all I had done was throw batting practice. I went in to Casey, and I said, "Casey, you're always givin' everybody a chance. I've always known you to be fair. The sportswriters have already told me I'm the unanimous choice to be sent out. I'd hate like hell to be sent out and not be given a chance to pitch."

I went out to throw batting practice, and he hollered at me to come in. I sat in the bullpen a couple of games, and then in the eighth inning of the first game of a doubleheader with Baltimore, pitching coach Jim Turner called and asked, "How do you feel?"

"I feel good," I said.

"Do you want to pitch the second game?" he asked.

I was so nervous and keyed up that the trainer couldn't even give me a rubdown. They were all kidding me in the bullpen. One of the fellows who was talking to me rather heavy was Jim Konstanty. He said he had been talking to the sportswriters and the word was I was going to be let go after the ball game. Because the Yankees had to make cuts on the deadline before they went out on the road trip.

I started the second ball game, and they scored off me in the first inning. Then I blanked them the rest of the way. Konstanty came in and relieved me, and he gave up a couple runs in the last inning, and they let him go and kept me.

I was packing, and I went to see Stengel in his office, and he said they decided to keep me. None of us knew right then. It was an hour or two later before they told us Jim was gone. I felt real sorry for Jim, but I would have felt sorrier for me.

I relieved in three games in an eight-game period, and I won three of them. We went to Cleveland, and Casey started me, and I won that game. Vic Wertz hit a home run off me in the second inning, but I beat Herb Score, 2–1. My wife said the three most beautiful things she saw in baseball was Ted Williams swinging a bat, Mickey Mantle bunting and running to first base, and Herb Score pitching.

When I pitched I tried to keep the ball in the middle of the ball field. Yogi was a great catcher, shortstop and second base were extremely strong, and in center field was the greatest athlete who ever lived. By keeping the ball in the middle of the field, no matter how hard they hit it, I had a great chance of getting somebody out.

I didn't overpower anybody. I liked to throw up and in, and I had a little slider that I threw outside, and to a lot of hitters, it didn't look like much and they tried to pull it, and they would hit it to center field. I wasn't a particularly heady pitcher. I was just an ordinary pitcher who happened to be with a great ball club at the right time.

I can remember one thing I couldn't believe, that I was going to start the fourth game of the 1956 World Series.

Ford got bombed in the first game in Brooklyn, and Larsen got bombed in the second game, and then it rained. Stengel came back with his best, and that was Ford. He was a little teed off at Larsen, and so at that time maybe he considered me his second best. I really don't know. These things just happen. Maybe he didn't think Larsen had put out the way he thought he should have because he was really counting on him to win in Brooklyn because he was a right-handed pitcher.

I ended up the season with sixteen wins, you know, had a real good season, and Stengel told me on the day it rained that he was going to start me in the fourth game of the series. I called my dad and asked him to come to the World Series. I told him I was going to start. My father was a National League fan, and he said, "There's no sense me flying all the way up there to see you warm up."

That was all the incentive I needed. I can remember in the first inning going out and trying to dig my usual toe hold in the front of the mound. I kept digging, but I couldn't feel it. Junior Gilliam was the first hitter, and I didn't get a ball close to the plate. On the first pitch I threw to Pee Wee Reese, Gilliam tried to steal second. It was a hit-and-run play, and that ball I threw as hard as any ball I threw, and I threw it right by Reese, who's a pretty hard fellow to throw a fastball by, and of course Yogi threw Gilliam out by a large margin. If it hadn't been for that, I might not have gotten out of the first inning. I walked the first batter practically in every inning. And I'd generally strike out the next batter.

I had a no-hitter for six innings. Gil Hodges, the first baseman, hit a single up the middle to score a run. In the ninth inning, we had a controversial play. Jackie Robinson hit a fly ball to left field, and Enos Slaughter lost it in the sun. Another hitter singled, and I walked a batter. Stengel came out to me. Generally, I was a 110-pitch pitcher. After that, he started looking for relief. I had thrown 145 pitches.

"How are you throwing?" Casey asked.

"Great," I said, and Yogi said I was still throwing good. On Yogi's recommendation, Casey kept me in the ball game. The Dodgers used two pinch hitters. Randy Jackson was the next batter, and Casey wanted me to pitch him low and away. And I pitched him the opposite of what Casey told me to do. I had ideas of my own. That was a reason I might have been a little hard to manage. But I had thrown batting practice to Randy when I was in the service, so I pitched the way I thought I could get him out. Pitching him up and in was dangerous in Yankee Stadium. I pitched him up and away. And up and in. I threw one pitch down, and he almost hit it out of the ballpark. And then I went up and in again and struck him out. I struck out the next batter and then I threw Gilliam a low fastball as fast as I could, and on the first pitch he hit a fly ball to Mantle in center field to end the game.

I was queen for a day. That's what they called me, because the next day Don Larsen pitched his perfect game.

After the series was over, Whitey told a sportswriter that if he and I hadn't won our ball games, Larsen would have pitched his perfect game in spring training. Whitey had a tremendous wit and was real sharp with words. The sportswriter couldn't think for a minute, and I never will forget, I giggled. Whitey was right. But Whitey could say it in a way that he could get away with it. If I had said it, it would have been smart-aleck. And I didn't have much right to be smart-aleck. What's the old saying, "Don't get gay when you're full of shit?"

During Larsen's perfect game, I was sitting on the right field side of the dug-out down the first-base line in the sun watching. I was basking in my glory of the day before, and I was sore and tired. I was elated, probably as excited as I could have gotten, but I couldn't get real excited because of my physical beating from the day before. I don't know. The

Don Larsen. Author collection

perfect game just crept up on me. Because Larsen was a marvel. To me, Larsen was like Mantle except that Mantle had more desire. But I believe Larsen had as much ability as anyone I've seen. Mantle had a deep love of the game. He was playing it because he loved it. Don didn't seem like he was playing it for the same reason. But by gosh, Don could hit a ball, he could field, he could throw, and he could run. Larsen was probably the third or fourth fastest man on the ball club. And he was a big man. He did everything with so much ease and so much finesse. Everyone said, "If Larsen would give a damn, he'd be so great." Well, they were wrong there. Larsen gave a damn. But he held it inside. Don was like the rest of us. He had all the great ability in the world, but his idea was, "If I win seventeen games this year, they are going to expect me to win twenty next year." And maybe he had reached a plateau where he wanted to be. He had the good money, lived the good life, he was with the Yankees, and he won enough ball games to stay in the rotation. But he didn't have the driving desire to be a thirty-game winner. Which I believe he could have been. In terms of natural ability, Turley and Larsen—you couldn't have picked two who had it any more than they did. As far as crafty, Whitey Ford was a tremendous pitcher.

I had an even better year in 1957 than I did the year before. I only had one complete game, but my earned run average dropped from 3.30 to 2.50. I didn't complete a ball game the second half of the season, but I was facing Dick Donovan, I was facing Bob Lemon, and it seemed like we were always having a seesaw battle.

I started the first and last game in Chicago, and I gave up a total of two runs in fifteen innings, and I didn't get a win or a loss. I was walking out onto the field to face Donovan both days. In the first game, we won 2–1 in fourteen innings. I went eight or nine, and we used a pinch hitter. I went out of the ball game 1–1. Ford had to pitch four or five innings to get the win. And it was 1–1 in the other ball game, when we beat Donovan in the 11th or 12th and Grim got the win.

"Dadgum, I pitched seventeen innings and I didn't get a win or a loss," I complained.

Donovan said, "I pitched twenty-five innings, and I got two losses."

Compared to him, I got out of it pretty fortunately.

In 1956, Mickey was named the MVP. Mickey was the player the fans came to see because he was so electrifying. You didn't know what he was going to do. He was strong, and he could hit one out of the ballpark, and he was so damned fast he was likely to score from anywhere.

Mickey liked western music. He just loved down-to-earth things. He would never say anything bad about anybody. It was what my wife admired most about Mantle. Even if she didn't like him. Mickey was a quiet sort of person in a crowd, but with his group he was a ball of fire, a lot of fun. He loved to giggle.

Mickey was visiting with Reba and me, and he was drinking Cutty Sark and water, and he was saying that there wasn't any kind of liquor he couldn't taste. And every time he turned around, Reba had the vodka and she would fill the glass. He was sitting there, and I kept talking to him and agitating him, and he was getting more loaded and more loaded, and he said, "Damn right, I can taste any kind of liquor."

By this time, his drink was 100 percent vodka. He started to get up and go to the bathroom, and he couldn't get out of the chair. He'd get up and fall down, get up and fall down. He said, "My ass is sure getting big!"

Mickey and I loved to play golf together. I think that's the reason I'm not on the Yankees now. We were horrible players, and yet we put it on the wall how many thousands of dollars we'd lose to each other every time we played. Jerry Lumpe was Mickey's partner, and I forget who was my partner. Lumpe was a bad golfer also. We were shooting in the neighborhood of 115, 120 and having a ball at it. The thing about it: if Mickey hit one straight, he'd drive the damn green, and the rest of us would be in trouble because it would take us six or seven to get there.

One time early in 1957 Mickey and I were playing at the Englewood Country Club. We were going into hole number nine, and I was one down, and we were playing for something like a thousand dollars. All we did was mark it on the board. The idea wasn't to lose money. The idea was to not get beat. This was just Mantle and I.

Mickey hit a beautiful drive, and he was off to the right of the hole. I hit my first shot and dribbled it down the way there. He was kidding me about my not being able to hit the ball very far, and he called me a little girl.

"Come on honey," he said. "Pull up your skirt. Don't let your bloomers fall around your ankles."

He was agitating me all the way up the fairway, giggling. I hit my next shot on the green, and he hit his on the green. I had about a thirty-five-foot putt, and he had a three-foot putt. And I sank mine, and he two-putted. And coming off the green I was going, "Heeheeheee." And it killed him. It made him madder'n hell.

As he was walking off, there was a tree limb hanging up there, and he had his putter, and he swung at the tree limb, and he wasn't quite high enough, and the club came down and hit him on the shin.

He was bleeding like a stuck pig, and I said, "Mick, we better go in."

"Hell no, we're not going in," he said. "We're playing the back nine."

All he did was wrap a handkerchief around it, and as he was walking, I could hear the blood going squish, squish, squish, squish, and so we continued play, and as it turned out Mickey won the back nine, and he was perfectly happy.

"What are we going to tell [trainer] Gus Mauch?" Mickey asked me. "And what are we going to tell the Yankees?"

He had won a Chevrolet station wagon for some reason, and I said, "Mickey, we're going to tell them we parked the station wagon on a hill, and you were getting in, and you pulled it out of park, and the sharp part of the car hit you in the shin."

It was a very serious injury. It went down to the bone. Mickey didn't do anything halfway. If you do it, you do it as a champion. He played like a champion. He took the abuse like a champion. Mickey didn't miss a lot of games either. He limped, but he played.

After I was traded to Kansas City, the Yankees came to town, and after the ball game Mickey invited me to go down and eat with him. We're eating, and he says, "Tom, you know you're the only right-handed pitcher that has enough control that I would bat right-handed off of you. I believe I can hit one completely out of Yankee Stadium off of you."

He was putting it to me the way it was.

"I'll tell you what, Mickey," I said. "If the ball game is not in jeopardy, I'm not going to take anything off of it, but if you walk up there right-handed, I'll reach back and let you have the best fastball I've got, letter high, right down the middle. And we'll find out if you're a better hitter right-handed or I'm a better pitcher right-handed."

"You're on," Mickey said.

Yankee Stadium. Author collection

Well, Eddie Lopat was my manager at Kansas City, and he had an automatic fine if he calls a pitch from the bench and you don't throw it. We were playing in Yankee Stadium and we got way behind the Yankees, and sure enough, in comes old mop-up man Sturdivant. And up steps Mickey into the batter's box as a right-handed hitter. And Lopat whistles to give me the curveball sign.

I tried to signal to him that my shoulder hurt and I couldn't throw a curveball, but again he whistles and makes a sign like he's going to fine me if I don't throw it.

The first pitch I threw Mickey was a big ole roundhouse curveball, and Mickey runs clear out of the batter's box. He is some kind of mad sumbitch. He gets in the box, and Lopat whistles again, and Mantle hears him. He walks up right-handed again because he's already committed himself.

Instead of throwing him a curveball, I throw him a slider—a halfway fastball—and he hits a line drive that center fielder Bobby Del Greco runs into the monuments in center field and catches it.

The deal was that he had to hit the ball completely out of Yankee Stadium or it was nothing. That was the deal, but anyway, it was caught. And he makes a circle and he comes running at me.

I wasn't going to stand on that mound and let that freight train run over me. And oh, he was mad, and everybody on our bench was giggling. Later on, he said it was one of the funniest incidents of his career, me throwing him the big curveball and crossing him up. Good ol' buddy, Tom. I want the truth to be known that I was told to throw the curveball. Like Mickey told me, I didn't have enough curveball that he couldn't hit it anyway. In fact, his exact quote was, "Throw that goddamn curveball, and I'll kill you with it."

And he tried to. Only thing, he hit it high.

After winning sixteen games in 1956 and 1957, I expected in '58 to have the same year, but I held out a little bit. I got mad because I didn't think I was getting paid what I should have been paid. And I held out. I didn't want to hold out. I wanted to go to spring training early, and I didn't sign, and when they didn't pay me, I got mad and goofed off.

And then I got hurt. Early in 1958, all the Yankee pitchers were running in the outfield. Bobby Shantz and I was half playing a game of tag, and we ran together, and I cut my heel, and then I hurt my arm.

It snowed opening week. I beat Boston 11–9. Quick as Mickey would hit one out, someone else on Boston would hit one out. He'd hit one out, and a Boston player hit one out. And I ran Mickey all over the ballpark. Stengel left me out there, and I stayed and struggled through it. It was a long ball game with a lot of hits. Mickey made a hellacious running catch for the last out. He brought the ball in and handed it to me, and he said, "Here kid, you deserve this ball!"

If I had had anything left, I would have hit him with it. He knew, of course, I couldn't throw hard enough to hurt him.

Jim Brosnan

It's a beautiful ballpark out in the sun, and the food is pretty good. Come out and enjoy yourself. Have a picnic at Wrigley Field.
And the players on the other teams usually did.

—Jim Brosnan

Jim Brosnan. National Baseball Hall of Fame

*J*im Brosnan was born on October 24, 1929, in Cincinnati, Ohio. He pitched in the major leagues from 1954 to 1963 for the Chicago Cubs, St. Louis Cardinals, Cincinnati Reds, and the Chicago White Sox. He had an up-and-down career, finishing with a 55–47 win–loss record. His lifetime ERA was 3.54, and he recorded sixty-eight saves. Throughout his career Brosnan, an iconoclast, was known as the Professor for his intellectual bent. Like Jim Bouton, he read books, not the *Sporting News*, and like Bouton, he wrote in great detail about his career in two popular diaries, *The Long Season* and *Pennant Race*. I interviewed Jim in 1995 for my book *Wrigleyville*. Brosnan played for the Cubs from 1954 to 1958, when the Cubs were a bottom-of-the-division ball club. He died in June 2014.

Jim Brosnan: In 1946, I pitched three shutouts in a row in an American Legion tournament in Flint, Michigan, and Tony Lucadello, who was a Cubs scout, happened to be looking at someone else on the other team when I beat them. He watched me pitch at Purdue and again at the national American Legion finals in South Carolina.

A week after my seventeenth birthday, he showed up.

"I would like to see you throw one more time," he said. "But I am prepared to give you $2,500 as a signing bonus if you sign with the Cubs."

I had never seen five hundred dollars at one time in my life, so I said, "Sure, where do you want me to throw the ball?"

So I got $2,500, minus $500 for the IRS, which wasn't enough even then to go to Notre Dame, which was my ideal. I was a good Irish Catholic boy who cried when Southern Cal beat Notre Dame. I went to Xavier University instead.

The Cubs had won the pennant in 1945, but I didn't know the Cubs were an atrocious organization until about my fifth year when Bruce Edwards, my manager at Springfield, Massachusetts, told me it was a shock to him that players in the Cubs organization had gotten to Triple A baseball and didn't know their fundamentals. He had come from the Dodger organization, which stressed fundamentals at every level. You knew how to play professional baseball after five years in the Dodger organization.

The Cubs had no coaching, no program, no method of teaching fundamentals to young prospects, and sometimes they didn't get very many prospects. It wasn't until general manager Wid Matthews hired Edwards over from the Dodgers that the Cubs started to have teachers in the various organizations. Before that, P. K. Wrigley hired managers because he remembered them.

"He probably deserves a job, and he can't play anywhere, so we'll let him manage one of our minor league clubs."

In 1947, I reported to St. Augustine, Florida, along with two hundred returning servicemen, who were guaranteed a shot at a job because they had belonged to the Cubs organization before they went into the service. I had number 172 pinned on my back. I didn't think that boded well for my future. *What am I doing here?*

"Don't worry about it," they said. "Most of these guys won't have a job when we leave spring training. A lot of them will quit after the first ten days."

Whatever talent they had was gone, and they decided to get on with their lives. And they would have been playing for very little money.

I played my whole first year in Elizabeth in Tennessee for $500. I got $2.50 a day to eat on the road, and I spent three dollars a day. I was losing money on food.

One of my roommates used to drive whiskey for [NASCAR legendary driver] Junior Johnson when Johnson was running moonshine. I only remember his first name: George. All he wanted to do was drive cars fast. He got on the old country roads. I never went with him, thank God. It's scary just thinking about it. He used to talk about outrunning the people who were chasing him, officials of the law or somebody trying to steal the stuff. He'd be going eighty miles an hour down the back roads of Tennessee.

I won seventeen games, and I was boosted all the way to B ball. Instead of $115 a month, they offered me $150 a month. For my seventeen wins, I got a $35-a-month raise.

That second year, I started out in Springfield when it was in the New England League. Bob Peterson was in his first year as manager. He had never managed before, and he had never managed anyone like me.

When I lost a game, it was suicide time. I went into deep depressions, and he couldn't figure out a way to handle that, so he finally got rid of me.

I probably had what they call bipolar, but just recently was called manic depressive. I was subject to mood swings, and being in the business I was in, the sport I was in, I could easily go from elation, almost manic elation, when I won, no matter whether it was a good win or one pitch in relief. If I lost, the depressions were always more severe than the ups. And they never heard of lithium.

Soon afterward, I had a year of psychiatric help, twice a week. George Moore, I'll never forget him, worked at the Institute for Psychoanalysis, which was the place to be in Chicago at that time. He treated all the problems I had.

I went to Fayetteville, North Carolina, where Frank "Skeeter" Skalzi was the manager in 1948. Old Skeeter and his wife, Jenna, were like parents, better than my parents ever were to me. I didn't have a particularly good record, but I did pitch a no-hitter. They passed the hat in the crowd and raised $175, which was more than my monthly salary. This was a home game, and a lot of soldiers from Fort Bragg came out to the ballpark.

The next year, I went to Macon, Georgia, Class A. Don Osborn, the Wizard of Oz, was the manager. He had pitched in the minor leagues for seventeen years on the West Coast. The Macon Peaches was an independent team owned by two businessmen in town. We only had seventeen players. You could carry twenty. At one point, we had fifteen, and Osborn got on the phone and called two of his old buddies, one a pitcher, one a hitter, from the West Coast.

We had a good ball club and won the pennant by twelve games. And Ozzy was an excellent manager. He was very good for me. The next year, he was at Nashville, and I got shipped there. He asked that I go down there. I was one of his protégés. I was a .500 pitcher, and I should have been better than that. I still hadn't learned how to pitch.

The Cubs had two young pitching prospects on the club, Umberto Flamini and me. They also had Jim Aslee, my roommate, who won sixteen games, and a pitcher by the name of Bob Spicer, who was about five-foot-seven, a bulldog with pretty good breaking stuff, and Osborn taught him how to throw a spitter—really a tar ball—a real good sinker. He taught us all how to pack our glove with tar and resin. If you put the ball in the glove and turned it upside down the ball would stay in the glove. If you knew how, the stuff could make the ball sink really good, like a spitter.

Aslee and Spicer were guys who most major league organizations had in the minor leagues, someone to win games but not considered major league prospects. That wasn't true of Flamini, who didn't give a shit about playing baseball at all. All he wanted to do was chase pussy, but he was left-handed and could throw hard. He could throw a curveball, but didn't like to. He just wanted to throw fastballs all day long. He was my age, nineteen years old. It was his first time away from home, some little place outside of Boston. When I went down to Nashville, I never heard of him again.

From Nashville, in 1950 I went to Des Moines, where Charlie Root, the legendary Charlie Root, was the manager. Charlie and I didn't get along from the get-go. It was just awful. A bad relationship. And yet I pitched very well for him.

I didn't know much about Charlie Root, except he had played with legendary Cub teams, with Pat Malone and Hack Wilson and all those people, though he didn't hang out with them. Root was a disciplinarian who didn't know how to do it. He knew a lot of guys on the club were fooling around, and yet he couldn't stop it.

Two things happened, and I'm to blame for one of them. Des Moines had two prospects, a third baseman and shortstop, whose names I have forgotten. The Cubs were trying to show their fans they had prospects, and they brought them up. The shortstop weighed 147 pounds, a little, bitty guy without much of an arm. Anyway, he wasn't a big league prospect in any way at all, but they took him up to the Cubs, and they took our third baseman who was hitting the ball well and driving in a lot of runs.

"It's a bad deal for us," I said, "because they're taking two good players away from us, and we're not getting anything in return."

Root thought that was a terrible attitude to take because here were two guys getting a shot at the big leagues.

"They deserved it," he said, "and we should root for them. You're taking a very selfish attitude."

Well, I was. I admit it. So I was wrong there. Root looked at me askance.

The second thing that happened, I pitched a game in Des Moines, and I was leading 1–0 in the ninth inning, and after an error and a bloop hit, we were tied. In the 12th a batter hit a ball, and our right fielder jumped up, the ball hits his glove, and it goes over the fence, and I lose the game 2–1.

Before the game, I had been reading the latest issue of *Time* magazine. I come into the clubhouse, sit down in front of my locker, pick up the magazine, and start reading it.

Root was enraged.

"How could you read that trash?"

He had probably never read *Time* magazine in his life.

"How could you just sit there and read it after what just happened?"

I had pitched very well and should have won the ball game. As far as Root was concerned, I should be pissed off, smashing my locker. Or crying. Or ordering a beer. Whatever. I should not be sitting there reading a magazine, and so Root wrote up a report on the game saying, "Brosnan has the wrong attitude and never will be a big league ballplayer." Right in the report Root said, "This guy has the wrong attitude. Get him out of here."

And he sent it in. And the Cubs brass said, "We have to send Brosnan somewhere else." But they didn't know where to send me.

I was fortunate because in the off-season I worked for Arthur Meyerhoff in his office in Chicago from 1950 until I wrote *The Long Season* in 1960. Meyerhoff worked for Mr. Wrigley. [He and Wrigley came up with the idea of the All American Girls Professional Baseball League, featured in the movie *A League of Their Own*. After the first year, Wrigley sold the league to Meyerhoff, who kept it running throughout World War II.] Meyerhoff opened his own advertising agency, and one of his clients was Wrigley Gum. I worked with Mr. Meyerhoff when he was doing the very first television commercials for Spearmint gum.

Meyerhoff knew I was going into the army, wouldn't be playing, and so he asked for the report to see what the club thought of my chances. He also knew Charlie Root. Meyerhoff had me come back to Chicago. He had to ask, "Is he still a prospect? Is he still throwing well?"

I liked Charlie Root's wife very much, and she was going to Chicago, and she volunteered to drive me, and I found her a very charming woman. In Chicago, I talked to Wid Matthews, the Cubs general manager.

Matthews pointed out to Meyerhoff, "He pitched a very good ball game. He pitched very well."

I should have gone into the army, but I wasn't called, and the Cubs sent me to Decatur, Illinois, the dumping ground. This was where all the misfits and oddballs in the Cubs organization went. Our manager was Morrie Arnovich, who couldn't tell he was handling misfits and oddballs because we were all like him.

This was B ball, the Three-I League, a legendary league. I don't remember too much about Morrie because nobody paid a damn bit of attention to him. He may have had signs, but nobody knew what they were. One time, he gave me the sign to bunt, and I hit a double. I didn't feel there was any point for me to bunt. But he wanted me to bunt anyway. So he fined me five dollars. Five dollars was a lot of money.

"I won't pay it," I told him. "You'll have to take it out of my paycheck."

Of course, he forgot to do that. In ten days, he had forgotten the whole thing.

Nobody on that club made the big leagues. At least half were college graduates in their second or third year. When you hit twenty-five and you haven't gone up, you're not ever going to go up. They don't want to take that chance.

The last weekend of the season, we were playing in Cedar Rapids. This young kid was pitching a no-hitter against us. I was losing 2–0 with two outs in the ninth, when up steps Bob Anderlik, a real pain in the ass. He bunts down the third base line and makes a perfect bunt to ruin the kid's no-hitter.

The kid picks up the ball and starts crying, and I'm crying with him. What a silly fucking thing to do. There were two outs. Our club wasn't scoring any runs. We weren't going to do anything. The next guy pops out, and I'm pissed at Anderlik and I tell him so.

Well, that didn't sit well with other players on the team. My roommate Bob Bortz said sarcastically, "This will go on your report. That's a good way to end the season, you big son of a bitch."

He ripped me up and down.

The next spring training, I went with the Springfield team in the International League because the army still wouldn't call me. I should have gone into the army in October, and here it is, almost April, and I wanted to be near home in Cincinnati, so I went to spring training. Which was when the draft call finally came.

The telegram said: "Uncle Sam wants you."

An ex-sergeant was in charge of my group, and he said there were three people to know in the army if I wanted to get by: the company sergeant, the mess sergeant, and the supply sergeant. Well, turns out there was another person even more important than they were: the special service officer, who when we were sitting down, asked, "Anyone here play professional sports?"

Frank Rogell, the Pittsburgh Steelers fullback at the time, raised his hand. Jim Bob Lemon, who played at Cleveland and Washington, stood up. I raised both my hands.

We have something going on here, I thought. Something obviously was going to happen, and it did. I was shipped to military replacement training, and Rogell and Lemon were sent to military police training. Which meant we had half the day off. I only spent half the day learning how to apply bandages and become a corpsman. I could have probably carried a stretcher, but that's all I could have done if I had been sent to Korea. The rest of the afternoon was off to play ball.

I didn't have to pitch. All I had to do was throw, and I could throw harder than anybody. I lost one game to Johnny Antonelli. He struck out eighteen. He pitched for the premier freeloading team at Fort Myer in Washington, DC. These were the guys who marched in Arlington and shot the rifles. They had five major leaguers on that club. And I lost to Bob Turley in an amateur baseball tournament. He struck out sixteen, and they ten-runned us in seven innings.

Most of the time I won. I won thirty-seven games in two years. We had a good ball club. We played eighty games a year. The only thing I got out of it was the confidence that I really did have an exceptional arm.

I came out of the army and went to Springfield in Triple A, where I went 4–17. It was 1953, and we had a bad ball club. We had a third baseman playing left field. The third baseman couldn't run. Sparky Adams was our shortstop, but he wasn't *the* Sparky Adams. He weighed 160 when the season started and by the end of the season he weighed 150 and his feet were gone. Ron Northey played right field. Ron was through at that time. It was Ron who gave me the nickname Reverend.

"Why?" I asked him.

"Because you look like a reverend."

I wore glasses. I was mighty happy when Frank Robinson called me "the Professor" because professor sounds much better and looks better in *The Baseball Encyclopedia*. Reverend wouldn't have looked so good.

I started, but I was trying to figure out how to pitch. I decided to become a sinkerball pitcher, because I remembered some of the tricks that Osborn told me about, how to pack resin and tar in my glove. But I never did really get it down. The International League was full of players from the big leagues coming down. They had been around. And they spread it around that I threw spitters, cause once in a while my sinker would really sink.

I went out there every fourth day, until I lost seventeen games. At first it didn't bother me because if I didn't pitch a shutout or hold them to two runs or less, I wasn't going to win. Then it got to me, and I intended to quit. The army offered a service. You took a battery of tests, and they'd tell you what sort of career you should get yourself into. I took a day off and went to Worcester, Massachusetts, to take the test.

"You should be an accountant or a writer," they said.

I didn't know any writers, so I decided to become an accountant, and the army got me into Benjamin Franklin University, an accounting school in Washington, DC. There were twenty-two students in the first semester, eight in the second. They weeded you out pretty fast, but they guaranteed you a job in two years.

I entered Benjamin Franklin just as the season was about to start. In my mind, I was through with baseball. That was it. My wife and I had been married since 1952. We had been at Fort Meade, living in Laurel, Maryland, and we had friends there. My wife was working while I was going to school. We were getting by.

In February of 1954, I got a letter from the Cubs saying, "You are invited to spring training, and we will send you a major league contract."

Which they did. I was to get the $5,000 minimum, but only if I stayed in the big leagues, $700 a month if I was sent down.

I went to spring training. What changed my mind, you ask? Five thousand bucks. Why not give it a shot?

And I made the club, despite the fact I arrived weighing 233 pounds, which was a good twenty-five pounds overweight. I loved to eat, and I looked it. I had assumed I wasn't going to play anymore, so I didn't work out.

I ran with the pitchers, and by the end of the workout I was puking on the sidelines. I'd run next to the fence and empty myself over the right field line.

I had shin splints. I never had a sore arm, but everything else that could go wrong seemed to. But my arm was fine. I threw the ball hard, and the Cubs had nobody else. Bob Rush got hurt, so they were short on pitching, and then I pitched a good game in Dallas on the day Phil Cavarretta got fired as manager.

"This is a fifth-place ballclub," Cavarretta had said to the press. "It's not a very good club."

And P. K. Wrigley said, "That's damaging to morale. You're fired."

Stan Hack took over, and he was one of the sweetest men on the face of the earth. He was embarrassed by what he had to deal with—his players. But he was determined to carry it through.

"If Mr. Wrigley says for me to manage," he said, "I manage."

Bob Scheffing, who was one of the coaches, was in charge of discipline. He had been an officer in the service. He could tell a prospect from a suspect, and the way I hear he told it—I got it from Mary Scheffing, his wife—I have to assume it's right, he said about me, "Every time Brosnan sticks his head out of the bullpen, somebody hits a line drive."

I had an ERA over nine. Pretty bad.

Howie Pollet was the pitching coach, and Howie decided he could help me. He not only was a helpful counselor, but he taught me how to throw a slider. And once I got the slider down, all of a sudden I could be a finesse pitcher, not a power pitcher. Before I learned the slider, I only had two pitches, a fastball and a change, and every time I stuck my head out of the dugout—bam, a line drive.

They sent me to Des Moines, and I pitched very well there. And I turned into a cheerleader. I talked to the younger players. "Let's go." My attitude had changed, and they loved it.

When Cubs pitcher Bubba Church got hit in the jaw by a Ted Kluszewski line drive, he was through for the year. Who are they going to bring up? *Moi.* To the great disgust of Walker Cooper, our backup catcher and pinch hitter. Walker simply could not understand it. I had already proved to him that I couldn't pitch in the big leagues.

We lose Bubba Church and we get this guy?

Well, even though I didn't pitch too badly, they sent me to Beaumont, Texas, and I pitched very well. I was 8–1. On the last day of the season, I was scheduled to pitch against Doyle Wade in the first game of a doubleheader against Shreveport, a team that had made the playoffs the night before. And they were all drunk.

I really didn't want to pitch. I asked our manager, Mickey Livingston, if I could cut out early. It didn't make any difference whether we won or lost. My wife was pregnant. I hadn't seen her in three months, and I wanted to go back to Chicago. I badly wanted to go home. In the first inning, I walked the first batter, and it looked like I wanted to get knocked out. It was a repeat of the game with Waterloo. This is the kind of guy you have to deal with.

Livingston came out and chewed my ass. But all they got was that one run, and that was it. They didn't get anything else, and we won the ball game 7–1. It took me fifty-five minutes. So why couldn't he let me go?

Right after the game I asked Livingston, "Now can I leave?" He wouldn't let me. I had to sit there and watch the second game. He was showing his willingness to discipline me.

After the game, I went to Chicago. I didn't care if I ever saw Beaumont or Mickey Livingston ever again. Beaumont was the hottest place I had ever been to in my life. Beaumont was a nice ballpark, but the mosquitoes were gigantic. Allan Russell, who owned the team, had said to me, "I'm losing money on the spray."

You couldn't get beer on Sunday. You couldn't buy a drink. You could if you went to one of the brothels. The girls, who were not tasty looking, talked baseball. They were fans. I went once. I didn't hit the sack. Ben Taylor, a big guy from the coal mines, and I had two beers, and we left.

The next year, I didn't get back to the Cubs. They sent me to Los Angeles, where I pitched for the legendary Bill Sweeney. He had been an alcoholic for twenty years, and it was beginning to show.

Bill didn't last long. The Cubs organization finally did something right when they sent Bob Scheffing to manage.

"I want to manage," Scheffing told the Cubs, "but at a high level."

So they sent Scheffing to manage the team, and we finished third. The next year, Bob won the Pacific Coast League championship. He had Gene Mauch playing second base, and Steve Bilko must have hit fifty home runs.

I was 8–7, and we were playing in Oakland, and it almost was a repeat of the Charlie Root game. I was winning 2–1 in the ninth inning. There was a man on first, and George Metkovich at the plate. I know Metkovich, know how I'm going to pitch him. I know where he hits the ball when he hits.

I turned around to face the outfield. Gale Wade is in center field, and I wave to him to move over into left center because I'm going to pitch Metkovich away, and he's going to hit a fly ball.

Gale Wade doesn't move. I signal, "Move over." But I had no authority to tell him what to do. According to Wade, it had to come from the manager. Or from Mauch, who was our second manager. So he doesn't move. He was a hard-headed son of a bitch from West Virginia, and he made up his mind he wasn't going to pay attention to anybody, especially me. He was pretty good, but he thought he was the best center fielder in the world. He even moved over to *right center* a little bit.

I threw Metkovich a high fastball, and he hits a high fly ball to left center field right in the gap, and if Wade had moved over where I told him, he'd have been waiting under it. So they tie the score 2–2. In the 11th inning, one of their batters hit a fly ball to right field, when a kid in the stands wearing a first baseman's mitt takes the ball right out of Bob Coates's glove. Coatesy was waiting for it. He could have reached up. But the guy reaches out and catches it. The lights aren't very good in the Oakland ballpark anyway, and the umpire at first base decided we had played enough. He said he didn't see it. I lose the game, 3–2.

On the plane ride back, I got so drunk on Gibsons that they had to give me oxygen on the plane. I couldn't sit down. I was wandering up and down the aisle on this commercial flight, annoying everybody.

The copilot came back and said, "We're going to have to put you off in San Francisco." It wasn't until after we were over Bakersfield that they were able to sit me down and keep me down.

My wife drove to the airport with Mary Scheffing. We lived in the same neighborhood in Hollywood. Everybody got off the plane except me and the two players helping me off. I can't walk. My legs are gone. They are carrying me. My wife said it was the most embarrassing moment of her life. She got back in the car to wait for me. The Scheffings took a cab home.

I got in the car and said, "Where is my baby?" My first-born came on March 18 when I was in spring training. The baby was sleeping in the back seat. While my wife was driving, I tried to crawl into the back seat.

"Sit right there," she said. "Don't move. I don't want you near my baby."

I don't remember the rest of the night, but the next day was pretty bad. There was nothing in me but little onions. Even today it makes me sick to look at a jar of Gibson onions.

I got to the ballpark, and Scheffing said to me, "Why are you here?"

"I'm going to get in the whirlpool and stay there for a couple of hours."

"You get in," Scheffing said, "but the trainer will tell you when to leave. Come back tomorrow. You're no good to us today. Tough game."

He sent in a report about the game.

The first line of the report: "Brosnan finally joins the club." He then went on to describe the game and what happened afterward. To him, I went from a sociopathic loner always by myself to suddenly one of the guys, especially the guys who drank. The social guys. And all of a sudden, I was everybody's friend.

I went 9–2 the rest of the year at Los Angeles. At the end of the year, we had a little party, and Bubba Church, who was pitching on our team, said, "Brosnan, you're the guy who's going to make the Cubs next year."

And he was right.

I was a rookie with the Cubs in 1954, the same year Gene Baker and Ernie Banks joined the team. They had both played for the Kansas City Monarchs of the Negro league. In the beginning, they were not accepted socially, but it was easier on them because they were both there. Both were quiet men, and all they needed was each other. They made no effort to be sociable. You wouldn't expect them to. Neither looked like they were going to be outstanding players.

Banks had nice hands. His arm wasn't very strong. He had pretty good range for a shortstop, but he wasn't very aggressive. His swing was smooth, almost effortless. You didn't notice that last movement of his wrist just before he hit the ball, how quick it was. Only in retrospect, you look back on it, and you said, *My God, those wrists are so fast.* The only player I saw who was anything like that was Eric Davis, when he was hitting all those home runs for Cincinnati.

Banks was the perfect guy to play first base. Greatest hands in the world. He handled the job at short, but he belonged at first base. He wasn't aggressive enough to play short or third. He was graceful but not quick.

Ernie Banks. Author collection

As I got older, I wondered why Ernie couldn't be more like Brooks Lawrence or Frank Robinson. They spoke up and had something to say that was worth listening to. Banks and Baker were more like Roy Campanella. I never heard them resenting discrimination and wishing something was done.

Baker was bright. He knew the game well, and he could make a double play. He had good range, not great range, good hands, and a second baseman's arm.

Gene could bunt, hit and run, do the little things a number two or number seven hitter could do. He was a professional, and he gave that impression right from the start. Much more so than Banks, who sometimes got down on himself if he made an error of struck out.

I spent 1955 on the coast, and then when I came back in 1956, all of a sudden Banks and Baker were the key guys on the ball club. Banks was hitting home runs constantly, and Baker was as good for the Cubs as Gene Mauch had been for the Los Angeles Angels the year before. Mauch had been a manager on the field. He really knew the game well, and so Baker suddenly became the team leader, even though he didn't get the press. And I don't think he got much support from the other guys on the club. We had Ralph Kiner and Hank Sauer and Frankie Baumholtz.

When Banks finally showed what he could do in 1956, he was embraced by the Cubs fans, because a Cub fan would embrace any kind of human being if that human being can hit the ball, catch the ball, throw the ball, score runs, and help win ball games, so it may have been easier for him than if he was with the White Sox.

And, of course, Ernie was the ultimate politician. Right from the start. It was almost impossible to get to know Ernie Banks. He would always say exactly what he was supposed to say. "It's a beautiful day. Let's play two." "Wrigley Field, the friendly confines." He invented that. He wouldn't say much, but what he said were clichés.

I don't recall having more than a couple minutes of conversation with him at any time.

It's hard to explain why the Cubs did so poorly in the 1950s. P. K. Wrigley and Jim Gallagher, the general manager, would say they were trying as hard as they could, but we usually finished last. We finished sixth once.

P. K. never worked things through in baseball the way he did in the chewing gum business. He was a very successful business-

P. K. Wrigley. Author collection

man. Arthur Meyerhoff told me that P. K. was talked into running the club, that it was a promise he had made to his father. He promised his father he would keep the Cubs in Chicago and never sell it to outsiders. Well, he did not run it well. He didn't pick people to run the Cubs for him the way he picked people to run his gum business for him.

Jim Gallagher, his general manager, had been a newspaper reporter. I don't think he knew more about baseball than the average newspaper reporter. They gave Rogers Hornsby the job of organizing the Cubs' way of playing baseball, and he was absolutely the worst person in the world to teach. He was *not* a teacher. He certainly was a good player, but a bad manager. He expected people to do things they couldn't do. Sure, every club should have a way of teaching fundaments. But just not him.

The people who knew talent on the Cubs don't get to pick the talent, and they compounded that by not having teachers, fundamentalists, in the minor leagues, to improve the talent they've got. I can't remember the last time they had four winning teams in the minor leagues. This year (1995) they didn't have any.

In the 1950s, the Brooklyn Dodgers were the dominant team in the National League. They were a right-hand-hitting club, and I was a right-handed pitcher, and I pitched against them. Duke Snider hit a home run off me in the eighth inning of a ball game to beat me 3–2. And I thought I had them beat.

I remember knocking Jackie Robinson down three times, and he never said a word. The third one was right in front of his nose. I was pitching him inside, but he stood right on top of the plate, so you had to back him off a little bit, get him off maybe six inches, and then you had a shot at throwing a strike on the outside corner. Otherwise, you had no shot at all.

Jackie stared at me—but he stared at everybody. But he never said a word, and I got him out. I kept pitching him inside, throwing a changeup away, and then I'd get the ball on his hands, and he couldn't quite get out in front of it. If it tailed in, he had to be ready to bail.

Campy hit a slider off me, just a bad pitch, into the bleachers in left center field at Wrigley, a real shot. Gil Hodges hit one, too. And Snider. Those are the only ones I remember. I remember the home runs.

The Dodgers were the best-hitting club. They were all veterans, and for a young pitcher like me, I would never get a pitch off the plate called for a strike, a perfect slider low and away. If I was facing Campanella, it was called a ball. But that's where you had to pitch him. For Hodges, you just had to hit the corner with a slider, and he couldn't touch it. I often wondered how he could hit thirty-six home runs a year if you can pitch him so easily. Then I began to understand: if he didn't swing at that pitch, it was called a ball. Only the veteran pitchers got that called, but it took years for a pitcher to develop that rapport with the umpires. Robin Roberts could pitch that far off the plate. Warren Spahn could pitch that far off the plate on either side. The last couple years that he played, Spahn didn't throw a ball over the middle fourteen inches of the plate.

In 1957, we had to face the Milwaukee Braves, another right-hand-hitting club. They had Hank Aaron, Eddie Mathews, Wes Covington, and Del Crandall. The one thing the Braves didn't do was play smart baseball. Johnny Logan would make all kinds of mistakes at second. And they didn't have much speed. Billy Bruton was the only one who could run.

I faced Willie Mays of the New York Giants. I had a good fastball, and I struck Willie out three times at Wrigley Field one day, twice on 3–2 pitches, something that had never been done by a Cub. He could have walked, but he wanted to hit the ball.

Willie got even with me. He hit a slider in the Polo Grounds. I could have sworn it went over the roof, but it hit on the roof. If it hadn't been for Dick Stuart, it would have been the longest home run hit off me. I was pitching for St. Louis, and Stuart hit one off me in Pittsburgh—this sounds apocryphal, but a guy came up to me the next day at the ballpark outside with the ball, and he said, "Would you sign this? This is the ball Stuart hit off you last night."

He found it in Schenley Park. He said he was sitting there, which is a good 500 to 600 feet away, and he said it was rolling. He was listening to the game when he saw it.

During spring training in 1958, Mr. W took me up to his mansion in Arizona. He had a huge mansion up on a butte overlooking the grounds of the Arizona Biltmore. It was his father's place. He pointed out his paintings, the various Remingtons that he owned. He introduced me to his wife, who was standing at the top of the stairs.

"This is my starting pitcher for opening day," he said.

"Yes dear."

She gave less a shit about baseball than he did. He invited me to go and see the rodeo. I went but I never saw him there.

I was named the starting pitcher on opening day because Bob Rush was hurt, and Moe Drabowsky and Dick Drott were serving their army hitches. I was the fourth pitcher on the staff, so by default I became the opener.

I had a very good spring training. Mr. W and Art Meyerhoff were at the ballpark, and Art invited me over for dinner.

"We'll go with Gus," he said. Gus was Mr. K's chauffeur.

We got in the car, and Mr. W. was in the back seat. Meyerhoff got in the front. I sat in the back with Mr. W, and he said, "Congratulations."

"For what?" I asked.

"You're our opening-day pitcher. I think you deserve it. Congratulations."

Then he said, "What do you think of my new idea about paying starting pitchers $15,000 a year?"

I had signed for $10,000 which was about what I deserved after three barely competent years.

"That's an excellent idea, sir," I said. "I really do. Thank you, sir."

Mr. Wrigley had a budget for his pitching staff. He was now paying $60,000 for the four starting pitchers, and that doesn't leave much of a budget for the other guys who had to be under ten grand or less. Cause that's the way he did things back then. Budgets. Seventeen percent of the money he took in went back into paying salary. Marvin Miller said so. Seventeen percent. That's what the players were getting of the gross proceeds.

Mr. Wrigley gave away radio and television rights. Talk about a bad businessman. He should have been charging for them. He spent a lot of money on marketing ideas that didn't work. Have a picnic at Wrigley Field. That was his appeal to fans who didn't know anything about baseball. *It's a beautiful ballpark out in the sun, and the food is pretty good. Come out and enjoy yourself. Have a picnic at Wrigley Field.*

And the players on the other teams usually did.

During the winter of 1957 we had moved into a house after I had gone to John Holland, our general manager, and asked, "John, am I going to be around? I need to buy a house."

"Of course you are," he said. You're going to be one of our starting pitchers."

Which I was—until May, when I was traded to the St. Louis Cardinals. I was a starting pitcher with a $15,000 contract, and they had to honor that.

The Cardinal general manager said to me, "Who do you know? You must have a friend at the top."

Because the pitchers on the Cardinals club were making much less. With better records.

P. K. did it for a year. A one-time thing. Just that year. That was one good thing that Wrigley did.

· 8 ·

Ted Williams

Baseball has been so great to me. I owe everything I have seen or
done or dreamt about to baseball.

—Ted Williams

The month of July has been declared Shoeless Joe Jackson month in his
hometown of Greenville, South Carolina. Jackson, a lifetime .356 hitter, was
one of the eight Chicago White Sox players banned for life by Commissioner
Kenesaw Mountain Landis in 1921 after Jackson and the other seven players
were cleared by a jury of throwing the 1919 World Series.

In the series Jackson hit .375 and made no errors. His twelve hits was a
World Series record until the 1960s. It's true he was given $5,000 in cash by
Arnold "Chick" Gandil, the Sox first baseman and the ringleader of the fix,
and it is also true that Jackson tried to give it back.

Over the final weekend in May 2001, the Central Florida chapter of the
Society for American Baseball Research met at the Plantation Inn and Golf
Resort in Crystal River, Florida, to hear Ted Williams talk on Jackson's behalf
to lift the ban and induct him into the baseball Hall of Fame. I spoke with
Ted that day; a couple days later, the phone rang at home. It was Ted. Could
I come over to his home in Ocala so we could talk more about Joe Jackson?
He wanted his thoughts broadcast.

"I'll be there," I told him.

I turned on the tape recorder. Ted, who died in July 2002, as usual was
animated and opinionated.

Ted Williams: Now why have I taken this great interest in Joe Jackson? It's
been kind of a slow, developing thing really. I have always been a fan of the

Ted Williams. Photofest

game, and after I came up to the Red Sox, I would talk to the greats of the past. Damn it all, it's too late, but I wish now I had asked other old players who saw Joe Jackson about him. Come to think of it, I did ask Eddie Collins, the man who got the Red Sox interested in me and one of the more respected men ever in the game. Eddie had played in that World Series with Jackson. Mr. Collins was always talking about the old players he played against—he couldn't stop talking about Ty Cobb, about Babe Ruth and Lou Gehrig,

Joe Jackson. National Baseball Hall of Fame

Walter Johnson and Lefty Grove, who played with me. But he never mentioned Joe Jackson, so one day I finally asked him about Joe. I remember it vividly.

"Mr. Collins," I said, "tell me about Joe Jackson."

He just dropped his head a little bit. Then he raised it, looked at me, and said, "Boy, what a player."

There was a reverence in the way Eddie said this that I had never seen before because he had told me about a lot of great players. And everybody I knew who had seen the old-timers said the same thing: "What a hitter!"

Ty Cobb told me he thought Joe Jackson was the greatest natural hitter he ever saw. And Babe Ruth said, "I tried to copy him."

I don't know what the hell more you need than that as to his playing ability! Great players were playing at that time—Ruth, Cobb, Tris Speaker, and whoever the hell they were—but Joe Jackson just might have been the greatest player of them all.

I don't regret much, but I do regret that I never got the chance to meet Joe Jackson. He lived in a little town in South Carolina, and the Red Sox used to travel through Greenville during spring training. When we got to that town, his hometown, I'd say, "This is where Joe Jackson lives."

Joe Cronin, our general manager who was one of the most beloved guys who was ever in baseball, introduced me to a lot of players. He introduced me to Walter Johnson. I got to meet Harry Heilmann through Joe Cronin. He thought Jimmie Foxx and Al Simmons were super players, and I met them. But he never did offer me a chance to meet Joe Jackson, and it must have been because of the feeling the world of baseball had against Joe.

You know the story. He was supposed to be one of the players who threw the 1919 World Series. And there may have been some evidence he knew the fix was in.

Nevertheless, the whole case has many shadows in it. The fellow was not very well educated. He came from that small town in South Carolina. He was brought into the fix by his White Sox teammates. He even told them one time, "I will not be in it." But they told him he already *was* in it, and when he threatened to go to the owner and expose them, he was threatened by Chick Gandil.

Joe tried to give the money back. He certainly did. It's all documented. He even went to the manager [Kid Gleason] and told him he didn't want to play in the series. But the manager made him play. They say Joe knew about the fix, but there were far more important people than Joe who knew about the fix. The manager knew. The owner knew. The press at the time said thousands of people on the South Side of Chicago knew the fix was on.

And Joe Jackson became the scapegoat. Joe didn't want to play in the series, and he tried to give the money back, but baseball wasn't interested in that. The higher-ups wanted him to be made into an example.

There is *not one bit of evidence* that shows Joe Jackson tried to throw the games. He swore to the grand jury he was playing to win, and if you look at the records, he hit higher than anybody, hit the only home run, fielded a lot of balls without making an error—had a great series.

When he went to court, he didn't even have his own appointed legal counsel. The club owner hired his lawyer. That lawyer wasn't there to protect Joe's interest. He was there to protect the owner. And after it was over, Joe

Joe Jackson and Ty Cobb. National Baseball Hall of Fame

still was found innocent of any wrongdoing, but baseball was in trouble. Base-ball had to prove itself, and the owners figured that Judge Kenesaw Mountain Landis should be given the absolute power to get the game back on its feet. The owners agreed they would abide by anything he decided, and Judge Landis suspended the eight, including Jackson, for life. His power in baseball was so great that nobody will ever have that much power again. He was given complete authority to pass judgment on the case. And he went against the courts! And it's eighty years later, and somebody ought to look at this closely and reappraise it.

I can remember my first really, really deep feeling about Joe Jackson. I was sitting at home looking out over the hills and meadows like I'm looking now, and I got a mental picture: on one side Babe Ruth was standing in the sky as big as life. On the other side was Ty Cobb, as big as life. In the middle was a kind of big thunderhead, and I visualized Joe Jackson there in the middle. Did I dream it? It is so vivid in my memory.

Baseball has shown it is capable of forgiveness. One of the current baseball owners [George Steinbrenner] was banned for life, not once, but twice, and he was brought back. Now I have to tell you, this man has done a hell of a lot of good in this game that not many people know about. So I'm not going to mention his name, because he deserves more than just that picture of him. But if he can be brought back, then Joe Jackson deserves another chance as well. If you look at the merits of Joe Jackson's case, you will see that the case against him has never been proven. I just wonder whether baseball has made a big, big mistake. Something as great or important or historical as baseball should not be too big to say, *Maybe it wasn't right. Maybe we should look at this more.*

Baseball has been so great to me. I owe everything I have seen or done or dreamt about to baseball. Baseball is so great, and I hate to think baseball could make such a big mistake against one of the greatest players who ever lived. Joe Jackson never got due process. Never, not even after he died.

The more I talk about it, the more I get mad at the game I love so much. What happened to Joe Jackson wasn't fair. I'll tell you one thing: this case deserves an awful lot of revisiting. Joe Jackson was banned for life, and now he's dead. To my mind, he has served his sentence, and it's time he be reinstated and given his rightful place in the Hall of Fame.

· 9 ·

Gene Conley

In 1962, I finished 15–14. I threw 241 innings and had an ERA of 3.95. But that's not what people remember. What I am asked all the time: why did I want to go to Jerusalem?

—Gene Conley

$\mathcal{G}$ene Conley was born in Muskogee, Oklahoma, on November 10, 1930. At Washington State University, he pitched on the baseball team that went to the College World Series and played well enough on the basketball team to be selected honorable mention to the All-America college team.

Gene Conley. National Baseball Hall of Fame

In August 1950, the six-foot-eight Conley signed with the Boston Braves for $3,000. In 1954 he made the National League All-Star Team and was third in the Rookie of the Year voting. He made one appearance against the Yankees in the World Series in 1957 and played for the Braves, now the Milwaukee Braves, through the 1959 season.

At the same time, Conley played professional basketball. He played for the Boston Celtics in 1952, quit the game to focus on baseball, and returned to the Celtics for the 1958–1959 season. He would play on three Celtics NBA championship teams. Because of basketball, he delayed reporting to the Braves for spring training in 1959 and was traded to the Philadelphia Phillies. That year, Conley made the All-Star Team for the third time.

As he relates, after leaving the Phillies in September a week early to start basketball training at the end of the 1960 season, the Phillies traded him to Boston. He played three seasons with a lowly Red Sox team but perhaps is best known for jumping off the Boston team bus in Midtown Manhattan with teammate Pumpsie Green on July 26, 1962, after losing a game to the Yankees and disappearing for a few days while attempting to fly to Jerusalem. Conley was one of only thirteen players ever to play both major league baseball and in the National Basketball Association.

Gene Conley died on July 4, 2017, in Foxborough, Massachusetts.

Gene Conley: Let me tell you the story behind how I was traded to the Boston Red Sox. I was with the Philadelphia Phillies in 1960, and my manager was Gene Mauch. Toward the end of the season, Mauch says, "Conley, I'm not going to pitch you the rest of the year. I'm going to pitch our young kids."

This was September and there were two weeks left in the year. I happened to be playing on a championship Celtics basketball team, and preseason was starting up.

"Gene," I said, "if you're going to do that, what good is it for me to sit on the bench and chew tobacca when I could be joining the Celtics and starting my basketball training?"

I was asking him to let me go, but he said, "Your job is baseball, so you can sit right here and watch these young guys pitch. We're paying you to put your uniform on."

"That's fine and dandy, Gene," I said. "I'd be glad to sacrifice my salary the rest of the year if you'll let me leave and join Bill Russell, Bob Cousy, and all these guys and get a good start in basketball for the season if you're not going to use me more. If you pitch me every fourth day, fine, then I'd love to stay."

"You're going to stay anyway," Mauch said.

"I'm sorry, Gene," I said. "I'm not going to do it."

"You're not, are you?" he said. "You better speak to the old man about that."

"I'm telling you right now. I'm not going to do it."

I went and got dressed right during the game, and I didn't join the team the last seven or eight days of the season. I thought about it, and figured it would not be smart for me to join the Celtics that soon. I did tell Red [Auerbach] about it. I figured I needed three or four days to rest up. It meant that much to lose my pay just to start off rested.

I went home to rest. I was living in Milwaukee. Would you believe I got a call from Bob Carpenter, who owned the Phillies?

"This is Bob Carpenter," he said. "How come you're not here with us in uniform?"

"Mr. Carpenter," I said, "your manager told me that I wasn't going to pitch the rest of the year and he wanted to give these kids up from the minors to pitch," and I mentioned to him since I played pro basketball that I felt it would be nice if he would let me have a little breather and join the Celtics, to start getting in shape a little earlier if he isn't going to use me.

"We're surely not going anywhere with this ball club we got," I said, "so I'm going to sacrifice my pay the rest of the year."

"Because you're a baseball player, we think a lot of you," Mr. Carpenter said. "We're counting on you for our future, but you're not going to do anything like this to disgrace my club or the Philly organization."

"I'm sorry," I said. "I feel bad about it."

"I'll tell you what I'm going to do," he said. "I don't want you to play basketball anymore. Anymore. Period."

I said, "It would take at least $25,000 in cash, tax-free money, for me to do that."

"I'll tell you what," he said. "I'll give you $20,000 not to play basketball."

"Oh, I'm sorry Mr. Carpenter," I said, "you're asking too much. How can I turn down the money I'm making in basketball? It would be very foolish. The only way you could possibly get me not to play is to pay me a salary on the side, but it would take quite a bit to do that."

I thought it over a little bit, and I said, "No, Mr. Carpenter. I have played a couple years with the Celtics already, and I'm in their plans. I might be able to play for four or five more years of big league basketball. That's worth more than $20,000. Even for $25,000, I'm selling myself pretty cheap."

"Don't give me any of this guff," he said. And boy, then he let me have it. He's Bob Carpenter, who was married to E. I. Dupont's daughter. They are the Carpenters and the Duponts, and I'm this Okie from Muskogee telling him what I want.

"Look, fella," he's telling me on the phone, "If you don't take my offer of $20,000, you not only will never wear a Philly uniform, but you will never pitch for me under any circumstances."

Now I know the guy is pissed at me. What kind of relationship can I have with this owner?

"Mr. Carpenter," I said, "I want to tell you something. I wouldn't give you the privilege of having me pitch for you anymore. You can take your Philadelphia uniform and stick it. I'm going to play pro basketball."

Before I could finish the sentence, he hung up on me.

So I've just lost twenty grand. The next day, I joined the Celtics.

"How did you get out so quick?" Red wanted to know.

"I got out a few days early," I told him. "It cost me a little money." And then I told him what happened.

"Bob Carpenter was born with a silver spoon up his ass," Red said. "You did the right thing. You ought to be proud you told him off. Now let's get busy and get in shape and have some fun and win another championship."

What a delightful thing for Red Auerbach to tell me. I felt so good. Red liked people who fought for their rights.

I started the season, and around the time it was nearly over, I get this call from the Red Sox saying, "We have just traded with Philadelphia. We traded Frank Sullivan to the Phillies for you."

I thought, *Fine, now I'm in Boston with the Red Sox and Celtics.*

Dick O'Connell, the Red Sox general manager, was a peach of a man. He knew Carpenter was so mad at me he'd give me up for anything, and that year I won eleven games with the Red Sox, even though I had arm trouble all year. But I won eleven games, and I thought, *The American League isn't near as tough as the National League.*

Don Schwall, a rookie, was our best pitcher that year. He won fifteen games, and the next year he had a couple bad games in the minors, and the next thing you knew, he went to work for a living. Warren Spahn once told me he always watched a rookie pitcher after he had a bad year.

"I want to see if he can bounce back," Spahn told me.

It's kind of weird. I first hurt my arm in 1955, and I can say this in all sincerity: in 1951, 1952, 1953, and 1954, and '55, I was one of the best right-handed pitchers in baseball, period. When I was twenty, I was the minor league Pitcher of the Year. When the Braves brought me up in 1954 with Hank Aaron, he was runner-up Rookie of the Year. They didn't pitch me for the first month that year, and I still won fourteen games.

I hurt my arm just before the All-Star Game in 1955. It was a Friday night, and Del Crandall was catching me, and we were playing Philadelphia, and Granny Hamner was batting. It was in July, and I threw an overhand curveball, and something popped in my arm, and Crandall heard it.

"What was that, Slim?" he said.

"I don't believe this," I said, "but something snapped in my shoulder. My fingers are numb."

I had been chosen for the All-Star Game, and it was coming up in a few days. I had an 11–3 record, and I don't know how I lost the three.

I stayed in, and they got three or four hits off me, and he took me out. I lost two more games before the All-Star Game. I actually won the All-Star Game, with nothing. I had the same numb feeling in my fingers.

The other day, I saw Ted Williams at a golf tournament. He was telling me, "I remember you pitching against me in that All-Star Game, you big donkey. You threw me that little curveball that wasn't enough to hit. You started me out with nothing."

I didn't have the nerve to tell him my arm was bothering me.

"You were looking for too much, Ted," I told him.

After that All-Star Game, the pain didn't go away.

Then they started bringing in the doctors. I had never seen a doctor before in my life. Never had a needle in my arm. They put needles here and there, and finally, and it's hard for me to say this, but I was such a valuable property, they told me to take the rest of the [1955] season off.

My record with the Braves was 42–43. I pitched in relief in the World Series against the Yankees in 1957, and gave up a home run to Mickey Mantle. I was 20–21 in my two years with the Phillies, though I did make the All-Star Game in that last year in 1959. My arm would bother me off and on.

In my three years with the Red Sox, my record was 29–32. In 1962, I finished 15–14. I threw 241 innings and had an ERA of 3.95. But that's not what people remember. What I am asked all the time: why did I want to go to Jerusalem?

It happened twenty-five years ago. [I interviewed Gene in 1987.] We were playing the Yankees in the stadium. Ralph Houk was the manager, and he was the manager of the American League All-Star Team. I had played in three All-Star Games pitching for the National League, with the Braves twice and the Phillies once, and I felt, *Wouldn't it be great coming over to the American League to be able to make the All-Star Team*. I thought it would be awfully nice. And I had nine or ten wins and was pitching a lot of innings, which was good enough for Ralph to pick me. But Ralph Terry beat me 1–0. We had the bases loaded with nobody out in the ninth inning, and we still got beat. I got beat by Bob Turley 2–1 in Fenway Park. So Houk knew I could pitch. Before the game, I thought, *If I could pitch a pretty good game . . . the son of a gun just might pick me.*

Well, as it turned out, everything went wrong. We made two or three errors. Carl Yastrzemski missed a ball in left field I could have caught, and he was the best left fielder in baseball. That's a tough field in Yankee Stadium. But four or five runs were let in—not knocked in. And I went out of the game around the fourth or fifth inning, and I thought, *That's the end of that, because Ralph's not going to pick me now.*

I was disgusted with the game. I was tired from sports. I was a pitcher so I had four or five days off, followed by the All-Star Game. After I left the field, I started drinking beer and by the time the team got into the clubhouse, I was pretty well smashed. Not falling down, but pretty well high. And I could care less.

Fenway Park. Author collection

We got on this bus to go to the airport to fly to Washington, DC, where we had three games to play before the All-Star break. Sitting in front were Mike Higgins, the general manager, and our manager, Billy Herman, real good people, real good baseball people and friends of mine. I got along good with them and with the players.

And we got into a traffic jam going across town. The bus was stopped on a street, and I saw a restaurant nearby, and I said, "I have to go to the bathroom." The bus had no toilet. I started up the aisle, and I hit Pumpsie Green, who was sitting in an aisle seat, on the shoulder, and I said, "Pumpsie, you got to take a leak?"

"Yeah," he said.

"Come on. This bus is going to be here for fifteen minutes. Let's run in here."

Well, we went into the restaurant, and while we were in there, would you believe it, the traffic jam opened, and the bus kept going—while we were inside this restaurant. When we came out, we discovered the bus was gone.

The driver could care less about us. He was probably hot and tired, and he couldn't just sit there and wait for us and hold up New York's traffic. So he left. I could have taken six guys in there, and they wouldn't have held the bus.

There we were in New York City with four days off because I was a starting pitcher. Pumpsie, of course, had to play. I didn't tie him up and make him stay in New York City. You follow me? All I had to do was chew tobacco and watch the Washington Senators play the Red Sox for three days and then I'd have a break at the All-Star Game, so I actually had five or six days off.

We were in New York City. It would have been foolish to go to LaGuardia and fly to Washington. The next game wasn't until tomorrow night.

"Well, we're here," I said, "Let's go downtown and have some fun. Let's do something different and perhaps we'll go to the airport later."

We went to Toots Shor's Restaurant. Toots was always nice. Every time I pitched in an All-Star Game or got into a World Series, he would send me a telegram and wish me good luck. Not that I knew him close, but that was the type of guy he was. When I told Pumpsie we were going to meet Toots Shor and say hello, he said, "Really? Sure, why not?"

We must have stayed with Toots for four or five hours. He hugged us both. The jockey Willie Hartack was there. Big celebrities in sports always came in there. Plus a couple of writers. Everyone was asking, "What the heck are you doing in town?"

"We just played the Yankees, and we got the day off, so we're just cooling off a little bit. It's hot outside."

I thought, *Who cares?*

The next thing I know, we were both pretty much smashed. We got a bottle of booze, checked back into the Commodore Hotel, and got our baseball rate again. I'm sure they were wondering, *Why are they checking back in again?*

We went up to our room and had a few drinks. We talked about baseball and sports. He said he had a brother, Cornell Green, who played pro football. While we talked we were half smashed.

"Pumpsie, I have an idea," I said. I think at this point I was too far gone. I said, "Let's take a few days off and go to Jerusalem. Let's get out of the country. Let's relax. The heck with baseball. The heck with sports, period. Let's just let them know we're taking a vacation."

"Oh no, oh no," Pumpsie said. "You're crazy."

"Come on, Pumpsie," I said. "What's the matter?"

"No, no," he said. "I don't know about you, but I'm going home."

We slept it off, but the next morning we were at it again. We had a couple of Bloody Marys and room service.

"I better be thinking about getting back," Pumpsie said.

"Aw Pumpsie," I said, "the heck with it. Don't worry about it."

I was about half smashed again. By that time, I was kind of out of it. I didn't have any money on me, but I had a few bucks in the bank, a couple thousand, so I went to the manager of the Commodore Hotel, who I knew—he knew me from the Braves and the Red Sox staying there, so I had been there a few years.

"Would it be possible if I cashed a check for a thousand dollars?" I asked him.

I was guessing that was about the right amount to fly to Jerusalem.

"I have to check with your bank," he said, and would you believe, the bank okayed it!

It was then that Pumpsie decided he better get back.

"You go ahead," he said. "Have a good time."

"You sure?"

"Yeah."

If he'd have gone with me, I'd have bought him a ticket, but at the time I didn't think about buying him one.

So Pumpsie left for Washington, DC. I walk down to Fifth Avenue and go to El Al Airlines to get a plane ticket. They gave me the ticket.

I had never been overseas or anywhere else, so there I am with my ticket in my pocket and a commitment that I was going to Israel. I had built it up in myself that, *Hey, I've gone this far. By golly, I think I just might go. I ain't hurting anybody. I'm by myself. I'm going to relax a few days. I've got a few bucks. How can I get in trouble?*

I go back to Toots Shor's and I'm telling everybody, "I'm going to Jerusalem. I'm going to Bethlehem. I'm going to go over to the Promised Land. I'm going to get everything straightened out between me and my Maker."

And they looked at me like, *This guy has three eyes.*

I started flashing my ticket around.

"Here's the ticket."

Well, there were people in there who knew I was a starting pitcher for the Boston Red Sox. They said to me, "Get a good night's sleep, and go to Washington."

"No," I said, "I'm not going to Washington."

From there, I went to Al Schacht's restaurant. Al was a former baseball player, and I had a good time in there. Well, the word was getting out that I was going to Jerusalem.

I said, "I'll see you guys. Because I'm going," and I called a cab.

I took the cab to LaGuardia Airport, and when I got there, so were the newspapermen. And there were photographers. And with them following me, when I got to the gate, I was told, "Sorry, fella, but we can't let you go without a passport."

I was so disappointed you wouldn't believe it. Because I would have to start the whole routine all over again.

"Aw, what the heck."

I got in a cab. I didn't want to show myself back at the Commodore Hotel, so I said to myself, *If I can't go to Jerusalem, I will go first class*, and I checked into the Waldorf Astoria Hotel. Why not?

I spent two nights at the Waldorf Astoria—first class. It cost two or three hundred dollars. I used a lot of room service. I sat in my room for two days as I started to straighten myself out.

I began to become ashamed of myself. Not afraid, but ashamed. *What have I done? What have I done? I have to have more pride than that.*

I couldn't call my wife because she was away at a camp for a week, so I got on the phone and called my folks.

"Son, where are you?" my mother wanted to know.

"I'm in New York."

"Are you all right?"

"Yeah."

"Do you realize you've been on TV? You're all over the radio. We're worried to death. We thought something had happened to you."

"Well," I said, "I'm a little bit ashamed of myself. I had a few beers."

My parents didn't know whether to laugh or cry. My father said, "Mr. Yawkey has called several times. He's quite concerned about you, son."

I said to myself, *Here you are, you big jackass. You're having a great year and you do something like this. Mr. Yawkey is a peach of a guy. Here he is concerned like I'm his son, calling all over. What am I going to do now? How am I going to face this? My teammates are either going to laugh or think I'm nuts or something.*

Oh, my goodness, what am I going to do?

I don't know how I did it, but I got in touch with my wife. She didn't know what was going on either. She had heard something in the news but hadn't gotten the full story.

"I'm coming home, and I'm considering quitting baseball," I told her.

Just a few days later I thought I might be going to the All-Star Game.

I took a train to Providence to meet her, instead of going to Boston, where I knew there'd be a lot of writers. I suggested we go back to her camp.

"I think you should," she said, "just to relax for a couple days and get back on the ball, get your bearings."

She was very sympathetic. Always has been. On the way to the camp we stopped to have a bite to eat at a little diner, and I could hear people saying, "Here he is." And I thought, *Holy mackerel, what have I done? They thought I was lost, kidnapped, or killed.*

I stayed at the camp for a day, and I said, "Katie, we got to go home. I have to figure something out."

We lived in a trailer in Foxborough, so we went back, and the trailer was surrounded by newspapermen, cameras, everything. I could hardly get inside. There I was, barefooted looking like an old Okie. They were trying to look in the windows, and we pulled down the blinds. I couldn't believe what was going on.

All this for going on a four-day toot, I thought.

I let in a couple writers to try to explain the story, but they couldn't quite get it straight. They didn't get the idea that I was concerned because I had arm trouble off and on, that I was thirty-two years old, which was starting to get to me, and the grind of playing both sports was tiring me out. My body was really getting tired. I had played four or five years in the NBA. I was ready to dump it all, but no one understood I had nothing to show for it. I had no future. I didn't have a college degree. I wasn't going to be a coach. After acting like I did, they weren't going to let me be a coach anyway.

So, I was just depressed, and maybe that's why I wanted to get away. And maybe I was getting a little religious. Maybe I was starting to see the light or something. I don't know.

I called Mike Higgins, who I really admired, and explained that I was ashamed of myself and was considering quitting.

"Don't be silly," Mike said. "Things like that can happen to anybody, and no one will even care. You haven't missed anything anyway. You're starting in a couple more days. So, you had a couple of bad nights."

I felt when we hung up the phone he must have been laughing. I felt that everyone was laughing at me. I was sure they were.

I called Mr. Yawkey. He wanted to see me in his office. He said, "Don't even consider quitting."

I had made a prepared statement that I was tired and it was time to get out of sports and get a job and work for a living and enjoy my family life. Most people have at least an off-season with their family, but I didn't have one, and I hadn't seen them in the summer for four or five years, so I don't even know them hardly.

That statement went over like a lead balloon with Yawkey and Higgins. They thought, *This guy needs help. Let's talk to him.* They didn't have to talk very hard to convince me no one was hurt, no one was ashamed of me, and come back.

It wasn't that I had to come back and win the pennant for the Red Sox, because we didn't have that good a club. It's that they were considering me as a person, and I thought, *Isn't that doggone nice?*

I decided to rejoin the team.

One final story about Pumpsie Green. I was with the Celtics when we were playing the San Francisco Warriors when they had Wilt Chamberlain,

Thurmond, and Guy Rogers. We were staying at the Jack Paar Hotel. I was on the elevator by myself, going up to my room, and this guy came on. He was about six-foot-four, 230 pounds, and he kept looking at me.

"How you doing?" I said.

"Fine," he said. "Are you Gene Conley?"

"Yeah," I said. "We're here playing the Warriors. What's your name?"

"My name is Cornell Green," he said. "I think you know my brother."

"Cornell Green, the football player? Are you trying to tell me you're Pumpsie Green's brother?"

"That's what I'm trying to tell you," he said. "What were you trying to do to my brother?"

We got off the elevator dying laughing.

· 10 ·

Kirby Higbe

There wasn't a lot of sense in fighting to keep Robinson off the team. Rickey was the boss, and he was going to do what he wanted to do.

We talked about it, but for me, that was it. Nothing we could do about it. We were going to play with him.

—Kirby Higbe

*K*irby Higbe was a twenty-five-year-old veteran pitcher when he was acquired by the Brooklyn Dodgers in a trade in the fall of 1940. In his five years with the Dodgers, Higbe had years of 22–9, 16–11, 13–10, 17–8, and 2–0 for an exemplary composite record of 70–38. His ERA was 3.29. Kirby helped the Dodgers to a pennant in 1941, and, he says, only World War II kept Brooklyn from winning more pennants during his time with the Dodgers.

Kirby, who was born in Columbia, South Carolina, was a Dodger when Branch Rickey promoted Jackie Robinson to the team in 1947. Higbe was among

Kirby Higbe. *National Baseball Hall of Fame*

the southerners who went to Rickey to implore the general manager not to add an African American player to the roster. It was not a coincidence that southerners Dixie Walker, the ringleader, catcher Dixie Howell, and Higbe were traded by Rickey a month into the '47 season, though Higbe contends that was not why he was traded.

My favorite Kirby Higbe stories came from his teammate, Rex Barney. Kirby had been in the army, and two weeks after he arrived home to reunite with his wife, Ann, a letter arrived addressed: "Mr. Kirby Higbe, Pitcher Brooklyn Dodgers, Columbia, South Carolina." The letter was from a nurse he was sleeping with off and on. Ann opened the letter and confronted her husband with it.

"Must be another Kirby Higbe," was his response.

Another time, Ann caught him in bed with a young girl. Higbe threw his clothes on, ran down to the bottom of the steps, and said to Ann, "It wasn't me."

I visited Higbe in 1981 for my book *Bums*. He died in Columbia on May 6, 1985.

Kirby Higbe: I went to the Dodgers for three ballplayers and $100,000, which was a lot of money in those days. In exchange, the Phillies got Mickey Livingston, a catcher; Vito Tamulis, a pitcher; and a kid named Crouch, a boy I pitched with in the Southern League. This was the winter of 1940, and this was what Leo [Durocher] said he needed to win the pennant in 1941. He told [general manager] Larry MacPhail he needed myself and [catcher] Mickey Owen, which MacPhail got.

I always liked Larry. He was a real showman. He was also real controversial. He and several fellows tried to kidnap the Kaiser during World War I. They weren't successful, but they made the attempt anyway. Some of the baseball people didn't like Larry too well because he'd outsmart them. After MacPhail bought me from Philadelphia, he was secretive about it because he wanted Owen, too, and then after he got Owen, he announced he had bought me.

In 1941, I had a real good record [22–9], and we won the pennant. The Yankees beat us in the World Series. That was the series when Mickey Owen missed the third strike, which everyone heard about a thousand times. Mickey was a real good catcher. That was just one of those things. He said [Hugh] Casey threw a curveball. A lot of people thought he threw a spitball, but Mickey said it was a curve that broke more than any curve Hugh ever throwed. Casey didn't have a great, big curve. He had more of what we'd call a slider. He was one of the best relief pitchers who ever lived. He and I roomed together three or four years.

I'll say one thing, Hugh was a real competitor. If you hit one real hard, he'd flatten you with the next pitch. Back in them days we'd have throwing contests and knock each other down quite often. Which you don't see too much today. I don't think baseball is as tough today as it was back when I played. I don't know how they make so much money. Of course, I do: television. They pay an awful lot of money now. Millions of dollars. Twenty-five thousand was the most I ever made. I wonder what I'd make today if I was in my prime. I'd like to try it one time.

Casey was a loner. Outside of me, he didn't care too much about messing around with other ballplayers. He didn't dislike them. I don't mean that. After a ball game, he would go up to his room and read a western magazine or a western book and smoke them big cigars.

When we trained in Cuba, Casey and I used to hang out with Ernest Hemingway. Ernest was a great guy. We'd go out every day and shoot them pigeons. They had pens in the middle of a big circle, and we had to shoot them pigeons before they got out of the circle. When you say, "Pull," they pull, and the birds fly up. They gave all the dead pigeons to the hospital. [Billy] Herman, [Augie] Galan, Curt Davis, Casey, and I and Ernest used to do it after practice

Hugh Casey. National Baseball Hall of Fame

every day. It was great. I liked Ernest. I really did. Quite a guy. That Ernest was some writer. He wrote "The Old Man at the Bridge." He said he done it hisself. He said he was writing about hisself. He said he was the guy who blew up the bridge. Of course, he was in the Spanish revolution. One time, Ernest told Casey and I that he had seen just about everything in the world.

Ernest was a tough son of a gun, a big fellow, boy. He and Casey hit it off. We had a lot of fun with him down there. Every once in a while, Hugh and Hemingway would drink a little bit, and they put on the boxing gloves. They'd start drinking, and they'd start fighting. I used to watch them. His wife was mad because they'd bust up the furniture in the house. He had a beautiful house up on a hill in Cuba.

Casey was the best I ever seen. When he died [in July 1951], I was playing in the South Atlantic League. We were in Jacksonville. Jesse Allen, a sportswriter from Atlanta, called me and he said, "What do you think?"

"What do I think about what?"

He said, "Casey killed hisself in a hotel in Atlanta."

"That's hard to believe," I said.

He killed hisself about his wife. He was talking to his wife, Kay. He was always crazy about Kay. He asked her when she was coming back, and she laughed, and he pulled the trigger. Damn, what they say is he took a shotgun and shot himself and blew his brains to the ceiling.

Ernest died the same way Hugh died. Killed hisself. Ernest and Gary Cooper were great friends. Not long after Gary died [May 1, 1961], Ernest killed himself [July 2, 1961].

We drew a million at Ebbets Field, and that was a lot of people in that 33,000-seat stadium. It was standing-room only. We used to have some battles with them Giants. I don't know why it was such a rivalry. It was more so between the fans than it was the ball clubs. We didn't have anything against the Giants. I don't reckon it will ever be what it used to be with the old Dodgers and the old Giants in the Polo Grounds and Ebbets Field. I was up there not long ago, and they got a big apartment building at Ebbets Field now. It looks real funny. You couldn't tell there was a field, but that was a real baseball town, Brooklyn. Los Angeles Dodgers don't sound right.

Leo Durocher was our manager. I'd say Leo was one of the best managers I'd ever seen. He could go in and make a talk in the clubhouse. We never did lose too many in a row when he was managing. Like he used to say, if his mother was playing shortstop and he had to break up a double play, he'd cut her legs off. And I believe it. Leo wanted to win that bad, and that's the only way to play. If you're going to play, you want to win. I know when I was with the Phillies (1939–1940), we'd get our brains beat out, and they'd go and congratulate the other team. I never did congratulate anybody who whipped me. I'd say, "I'll get you next time." But as far as shaking hands and congratulating someone who did you bad, I never believed in that. And I don't think Leo did either. He said, "We'll get 'em tomorrow boys. Don't fraternize with the enemy on the field. You want to take them out for a steak after the ball game, take them, but don't talk to them during the ball game." It was like war. When I was pitching, Leo would say to me, "Don't ever let them take the bread and butter out of your mouth."

He was right. You go out to win. I ain't never seen a loser who didn't lose a lot of times. And the thing is, they enjoy it. They shake hands after you beat their brains out. I never believed in that.

The only thing about Leo, he overmanaged sometimes. After we won the pennant in '41, Leo pitched me about one inning a week. Going into the 1941 World Series, I was the winningest pitcher he had, but I wasn't in shape, and he didn't pitch me until the fourth game. He started Curt Davis in the first game at Yankee Stadium and Whitlow Wyatt in the second. That was great. Wyatt was a real pitcher. He was 22–10. I was 22–9. But then in the third game, I was sure I was going to pitch, but he pitched Freddie Fitzsim-

Leo Durocher. Author collection

mons instead of me. The score was 0–0 in the seventh inning when Freddie got hit in the knee with a line drive. Hugh Casey then gave up two runs, and we lost 2–1.

When Leo didn't pitch me in Game 3, I got mad.

"I don't care whether I pitch or not, really," I told him.

I hadn't thrown in a while. When you're used to pitching every day and you don't throw for two weeks, it gets a little rough. I gave up a run in the first and two in the fourth, and Leo took me out. We lost when Mickey Owen didn't catch Hugh Casey's third strike. The Yankees went on to win the game and the series.

We didn't win the pennant in '42 and '43. That's when the war started. We lost some pretty good ballplayers in '42, and I left in '43.

We'd have kept winning except for the war. We had Pee Wee Reese and Dixie Walker and Joe Medwick, a nucleus of a good ball club, and if it hadn't been for the war, we'd have won the pennant for a few more years. The Cardinals sure didn't lose as many men as the Dodgers lost to the service.

I went right into the infantry, the 42nd. You talk about baseball players getting preferential treatment. I never did get it. I was in a combat unit. I went to the Pacific. The war was halfway over when I went over there. There was nothing funny about the war. It shortened my career. I missed two whole years. When I came back to Brooklyn in '46, I came to spring training late. It made a difference. Hand grenades and baseballs are a little bit different.

In '46, I won 16 and lost 8. I won my first nine in a row. We had Cookie Lavagetto at third, Reese at short, Billy Herman at second, and old Dolph Camilli at first. You couldn't have a better infield. The Cardinals came close with Kurowski and Marion and Schoendienst, though the Cardinals didn't have a great first baseman. As for Camilli, there never was an equal in baseball. He could dig 'em out of the dirt. He never did flinch. He didn't get out of the way. Dolph was some ballplayer.

The Cardinals were bigger rivals than the Giants. We used to fight with them all the time. Old Mort Cooper was a pretty good pitcher. They had Ernie White and Howie Pollet. I tell you we respected that ball club back in those days. Of course, they had Musial and Slaughter and Terry Moore in the outfield. Moore, the center fielder, played right behind second, and he'd go back and get them off the wall. I tell you, we had some pretty good battles. Our man, Pete Reiser, was so good in the outfield. He could go get that ball. If he hadn't run into that wall, he'd have lasted a long time. Walls didn't make no difference to him. Pete ran into so many walls, that's why they put in the warning track in the outfield. So you know when you get close to that wall.

In '46, we tied for the pennant with the Cardinals, and we lost in a playoff. Then in 1947, the Dodgers began spring training in Havana, Cuba.

Havana was some place, boy. It never did rain. We hung out with Ernest. That was about the best place I'd been to for spring training, though I have to say I hated the food. We stayed at that big hotel, the Nacional, and we spent a lot of time in the casino. We played games against Montreal, our farm team. Jackie Robinson was playing for Montreal, and Branch Rickey was talking about bringing him up.

Because of Robinson we had spring training in Cuba, Venezuela, and Panama. In Panama, Dixie Walker, myself, Carl Furillo, Pee Wee Reese, and Dixie Howell, the catcher, went to see Branch Rickey. Dixie, Pee Wee, and I were good buddies. We would run around together a lot. Pee Wee was a great ballplayer. Everyone we had on the team liked him, no doubt about it.

We talked to Branch Rickey and said we didn't want to play with Robinson. Furillo *was* one of them. I don't know if someone influenced him or not. I don't know if Reese backed down, because Reese said that Jackie was a real good guy. [Both Furillo and Reese steadfastly deny they were part of the group who went to see Rickey about not wanting to play with Robinson.]

Not that we objected that much to playing with him. We all went together to tell him, and nothing really happened. We just told Rickey we'd rather not do it. We didn't come out and say we weren't going to play. We said, "We're rather you didn't bring him up." Rickey said he was, and that was all there was to it. What else could be said?

The way Rickey handled things, he said, "If you want me to trade you, I'll trade you." None of us said we wanted to be traded. There was a lot of bad publicity about it, which wasn't right. There wasn't a lot of sense in fighting to keep Robinson off the team. Rickey was the boss, and he was going to do what he wanted to do.

We talked about it, but for me, that was it. Nothing we could do about it. We were going to play with him.

I grew up in Columbia, South Carolina. My grandfather fought for the South, and my other grandfather fought for the North. He fought for the North because he was from Ohio. He ran away from home and came down here and married my grandmother. The medics wanted to cut his leg off, and he told them, "If I'm going to die, I'm going to die." His leg was in bad shape, but he never lost it. He had a limp all his life. He could tell some stories about dropping some biscuits into that coffee [during the Civil War], and the worms would come to the top, and he'd eat the worms. He talked about nearly freezing to death half the time. He said it was just horrible. That was the worst war we ever had, brother fighting against brother and uncle against uncle.

I never did know my other grandfather who fought for the South. He died before I was born.

Back then there was no problem between whites and blacks that I know of. My daddy worked in a company. We had a maid named Becky. We used to call her Becky Higbe. As I said, we never had any problems with the blacks.

I think most of the trouble came up North, the way they treated the colored up there. When I was with the Dodgers, I ran into a lot of colored people that I talked to in Brooklyn, and they said that if they got any money, they were coming back down South. They liked it better in the South than they did in the North. But if you listened to the people in the North, you'd have thought we treated the blacks terribly. Some friends up there asked me, "Why don't you treat the blacks better?"

We never treated them bad in my life that I ever seen. They *were* segregated. I reckon that was an old southern custom. We had colored come to our church when I was going to the Baptist church growing up as a boy. We never objected to them coming to church.

I got numerous letters from down South about my playing with a colored fella. "How can you do it?" and stuff like that. I wrote back and said, "If you pay me $25,000, I won't play with him." But I didn't get any offers. Nobody really put any pressure on me, but you could see it coming to that, so why not adjust to it? It's like being in the service. If you're in combat you have to adjust. If you don't, you go crazy.

I think Robinson coming up changed baseball dramatically. He was a great athlete, no doubt about it. He did have to go through a lot because they didn't treat him too good. At least 50 percent of the players were southerners, and they weren't too happy. They did knock him down. But he was up to the task. He could handle it. He was just that kind of guy. Jackie was just one hell of an athlete.

I remember in 1947, the commissioner came around and said, "The beanball is out. You can't throw it anymore."

Leo asked, "How in the world do you know if he's throwing it on purpose?"

"I can tell when a big league pitcher is throwing a beanball," he said. "They aren't that wild."

And I guess he was telling the truth. They put that in because of Robinson. They had to, really. After Don Newcombe and Dan Bankhead joined the Dodgers, he didn't get thrown at as much, though Bankhead wasn't much of a pitcher.

I was only there in Brooklyn a short time in '47. Almost a month. It wasn't that bad playing with Robinson. I won my first two starts, and then I was gone. I had to leave a great ball club. I got traded to Pittsburgh.

When I was traded, I asked Rickey, "Was that on account of Robinson?"

He said, "No, you said you were going to play. But you only have a couple more years. [On May 3, 1947, Rickey traded Higbe, Hank Behrman,

Dixie Howell, and Cal McLish to Pittsburgh for Al Gionfriddo and $100,000. He would trade Dixie Walker to the Pirates at the end of the season.]

In '46, I was with a first-place team. In '47, I played for Billy Herman, who was all right as a manager, but who wasn't very good when it came to handling men. In '48, I played for Billy Meyer, and then in '49 I was back in New York with the Giants. But I didn't pitch much. Of course, I was over the hill anyway. My best years were with the Dodgers. Leo had become the Giants manager, and he asked me if I would go to Minneapolis. I said I reckon so. I liked to quit right then, but I liked the game so much. Minneapolis was a good baseball town.

Before I left the Giants, Leo said to me, "I'm going to bring up a guy tomorrow who is going to be the best ballplayer in the National League." I had never heard of Willie Mays.

Leo turned out to be right.

Phil Rizzuto

In 1950, I won the Most Valuable Player Award, but then after DiMaggio left after the 1951 season, I was the last of the old guard left. Casey wanted all of the old-timers out so he could get all the young kids so he could let them know who was boss.

—Phil Rizzuto

The Scooter, Phil Rizzuto, was born on September 25, 1917, in Brooklyn, New York. He was the son of a streetcar motorman and his wife, both of whom emigrated from Calabria, Italy. Rizzuto, who was only five-foot-six, starred for the New York Yankees for thirteen years from 1941 to 1956. His play was interrupted by World War II from 1943 to 1945.

Phil, a shortstop whose play solidified the Yankee infield for more than a decade, played on seven Yankee World Series winners, and in 1950 he was named Most Valuable Player of the American League. He famously was let go by the Yankees in the middle of

Phil Rizzuto. National Baseball Hall of Fame

the 1956 season at the Old-Timers' Game, but because he held his tongue, later that year he was offered a position with the Yankee announcing team

115

alongside Mel Allen and Red Barber. Rizzuto was a fixture on TV and radio, retiring in 1996 after forty years in the booth. His partnership with Bill White entertained Yankee fans for a generation.

The Yankees retired Rizzuto's number 10 in 1985, and he was elected to baseball's Hall of Fame in 1994. He died on August 13, 2007, at the age of eighty-nine. I interviewed him in 1974 at Yankee Stadium for my book *Dynasty*.

Phil Rizzuto: It was always tough to get a baseball when we were kids. Nobody had enough money. When the cover would wear off the baseball and the stitches would break, we would take the cover off and stuff it with rags and then resew the baseball by hand. The pitcher would then be able to throw as hard as he wanted, curveballs, fastballs, anything, and you would hit with a regular bat, and that helped me more than anything else in learning how to hit good pitching, even though I was small. My experience was so much better than what kids in Little League get now, where the one pitcher who is overpowering usually is the mainstay of the team.

When I was a kid, they didn't have the Little League fields or the equipment that they have today. I was born in Ridgewood in Brooklyn, so we played most of our baseball on the streets and on whatever sandlots were available. Today, with everything organized, you know how kids are, if it isn't organized, they won't play by themselves.

Joe Kress and I were great buddies. He lived in my neighborhood, close to the Jamaica Line, near the cemetery. Joe was with the Bushwicks for a long, long time. In 1936, when I was still in high school, he gave me some money to play, and I played against Satchel Paige and those Black Yankees. We played the Kansas City Monarchs, and that was better than any minor league experience you could get. I played against Josh Gibson, the great catcher. Max Robinson would put the balls in the ice box because when a ball is cold, they couldn't hit it as far. We used those balls when the opposing team was up, and we used the regular balls when the Bushwicks were up. Because I was still in high school, I played under an assumed name, an Irish name. I was Phil Murphy. I even played with the Bushwicks in 1937 for a few dollars after my first year in the minor leagues. I also played for Gene Barton's Nighthawks. Barton was a great actor. I was sixteen years old when I played for them.

While I was in high school I had a tryout with Brooklyn. Casey Stengel, their manager, was there. I remember very well what he said to me.

"You're too short, kid," he said. "You ought to go out and shine shoes. You can go in the stands and watch the game, but you will never be a big league ballplayer."

In those days, they had so many minor leagues. They were looking for the big ballplayers who could hit the ball out of the park. Here I was from Brooklyn. The Dodgers were always my favorite team, and I had a tryout with them. The only guy who was nice to me was Tony Cuccinello. I used to bring this up to Casey a lot. He and I never got along that well anyway.

Joe Kress was instrumental in getting me signed by the Yankees. I was seventeen when I signed to go to Bassett, Virginia, and I went away.

It was the first time I had ever been away from home in my life. Here I was, a fellow from Brooklyn who had never been out of Brooklyn in his life, who suddenly finds himself on a train going to Virginia, which I thought was like going to Europe.

I'll never forget that train trip. The Yankees didn't give any bonuses or expense money. You had to pay your own way down there. My father had given me a ten-dollar bill. He pinned it to the inside of my undershirt. The Mafia used to put the Black Hand on you. My father, being from Calabria, Italy, was scared to death of me traveling. I had to sit up the whole trip. He was afraid somebody was going to steal my money. My dad had never been away. He came from Italy, but he never left Brooklyn.

Our first stop on the train was Roanoke, Virginia, and I never will forget, we got off the train, and I had southern fried chicken for the first time. It was delicious.

And then we got to Bassett. I got off the train, and I saw nothing but hills. Absolutely nothing, and when the train pulled away, there was the town. There, on the other side of the train, was a drug store, a theater, a little hotel, and a diner. I couldn't believe it. Imagine all the hustle and bustle of Brooklyn, and to come to something like this! It took me a long time to get used to it.

When I got to Virginia, it was a whole new world. I didn't understand them and they didn't understand me. I really had a Brooklyn accent. Those southerners, I couldn't understand them. I'll tell you, it was frightening.

But again, I was lucky. Ray White, who had gone to the same high school I went to, Richmond High School, was the manager. I had played with Ray in semipro ball when I was playing under the assumed name of Phil Murphy. So, Ray White knew my capabilities. There were several other shortstops trying out. Naturally, he kept me.

My career almost ended at Bassett. Running down to first base, I stepped in what they call a gopher hole. I played for about three weeks after that, and every night I was in agony. But when you're in a D league, you don't have a trainer. The manager is the trainer, the bus driver, the secretary, everything because you drive to the town, play, and come back the same night. Ray used to rub my leg every night and pound it.

Finally, it got so bad, an old umpire one night in Bassett saw I was in pain, and he said, "Kid, you better have that thing looked at."

Ray White the next day took me to Roanoke, the only big town that had a hospital anywhere near, and the doctor examined me and said, "We have to operate on you—immediately." Here I was, eighteen years old, scared to death. They had to call my mother and tell her, and she drove down with my Uncle Mike and my brother the next day. So, they operated on me immediately, and when I came to—remember in those days they didn't have penicillin or pentothal. They had to give me either ether or gas, and when I woke up I was throwing up, and my whole leg was bandaged.

"In another week, you'd have lost your leg," the doctor told me.

Turned out, gangrene had set in and had eaten away much of a muscle. They had to cut all that dead muscle away, and he sewed each end on to another muscle, and I have a scar on my leg from my knee to my thigh. It's still an ugly looking thing.

That happened after a month and a half of the season, and then I missed the next two and a half months, and then I finished the season. I had a good year. I hit .310, and we made the playoffs and won the championship.

But as I say, I was very, very lucky.

The next year, I was promoted to Norfolk in the Piedmont League. Ray White was promoted from Bassett to Norfolk, and he took me with him.

Phil Rizzuto. Photofest

I made it to the Yankees in 1941, and we won two World Series before I entered the navy. In the spring of 1946, I had just come back from three years in the service, and I was finding it tough to get back into the groove. I hadn't faced good pitching, and I had only played that one year in 1943. In 1944 and 1945, I was in New Guinea, Australia, and the Philippines. So, when I came back in 1946, I couldn't quite pick it up. I figured I had had it. Every year I played in the minors and in the two years I had played with the Yankees, I had hit .300, and here I was batting .256, which is good today but in those days wasn't very good. I just didn't have the rhythm, and it was around this time when the Pasqual brothers from Mexico were trying to get major leaguers to play in Mexico.

If you remember, after 1942 the owners froze all the salaries. I had a good year in 1942 but I didn't get a raise. When I came back in '46, I had to take what I was paid in 1942. Things were tough. You couldn't get cars. You couldn't get butter. You couldn't get nylons. So, the Pasqual brothers were flashing around a lot of money, and it was Al Gardella, Danny Gardella's brother, who approached George Stirnweiss and myself. He had approached Stan Musial, and he had signed Junior Stephens and Sal Maglie.

So, George and I had a meeting with Jorge Pasqual. We sat in his big Cadillac, and he slipped out ten thousand dollars and offered it to George and I.

"Take this and we'll talk about it," he said.

It was very tempting, because ten thousand dollars in 1946 was *a lot* of money.

He took to dinner George Stirnweiss and his wife, and me and Cora at the Waldorf or the Roosevelt, one of the big hotels in New York, and Jorge and Bernardo Pasqual were telling Cora how they could get her butter and nylons, that they would buy George and me apartment houses in Mexico City and give each of us $50,000 a year. That was *a lot* of money. You couldn't help but listen.

The Pasquals were big men in Mexico. I really don't know what they did. [They were sons of a wealthy shipping magnate.] They had a lot of money, and all the time they carried guns. One of them was killed in a shootout several years later.

Jorge Pasqual said, "Come on. We'll drive right to Mexico tonight."

We were each to get a new Cadillac, and when we got to Mexico we were supposed to call Joe McCarthy and tell him.

"No," I said, "Joe has been good to me. I want to call and tell him before we go."

In the meantime, my wife, Cora, wanted nothing to do with it. She's a true-blue American all the way. And it's a good thing. I was looking at the money, the future for our family, and as I said, I thought I had had it. I wasn't playing the way I used to play. But she had the common sense.

We didn't know it, but MacPhail had bugged Pasqual's room. It had to be bugged because they knew what was going on. We didn't know. Imagine, in those days. You talk about Watergate!

The next day, Larry MacPhail called George Stirnweiss and I into his office. Larry said they had heard the whole thing, and he told us we had to testify against the Pasquals.

"We don't want to testify," George and I both said. "He wants to help us out. He's trying to give us more money."

George and I were both suspended for about three days.

When the case was to come to court, the Pasquals left town. George Weiss came over to my apartment. At the time, I lived in an apartment in Hillside, New Jersey. I was getting ready to go to Mexico, and George tried to talk me out of it. But then the case came up, and the Pasquals left town, and they lifted the suspension, and the very next day they gave me a raise.

And everything turned out to be a bed of roses for me. I could very well have been in the same boat as Sal Maglie and the others who went. The league lasted a year, and anyone who went to Mexico was barred from playing for five years. And whatever the money they made in Mexico, the IRS grabbed them, and they had to pay the taxes. So, I was lucky. If it hadn't been for my wife, I'd have gone.

Joe McCarthy called me and told me what had happened to him. He had jumped from the minors to the Federal League [in 1914], after they had wined and dined him, and that league had folded, and from his experience he told me I was very lucky.

McCarthy wasn't fond of Larry MacPhail, one of our three owners, because MacPhail was like Charlie Finley.

He tried to get involved in running the ball club. In all the years he had managed, McCarthy never had a problem, but whenever MacPhail wanted to get involved, Joe wouldn't stand for it. MacPhail tried telling him who to play, but he wouldn't go for it. It was one of the reasons Joe had so many problems in 1946. Joe got sick a couple times. He was drinking heavily, which happened one month every three years. One time they locked him in the clubhouse during a game. When he did drink, which wasn't that often, he was an angry drunk.

He had a big argument with Joe Page on the airplane going to Detroit. Joe picked on Page because Page liked to hit the bottle quite a bit. The writers were there, and they blew it all out of proportion. They put a lid on Joe's coffin. The writers didn't like McCarthy, didn't like managers like him. Writers needed stories, and Stengel would give them to them. But Joe wasn't that type. When asked why he did something, Joe would knock them down verbally a lot. They didn't like him, and any chance they got to really stick it to him, they did.

It was in the middle of the season, if you remember. As far as I know, they fired him. And Bill Dickey was made manager, and it was a shame that didn't work out. As great a player as Bill was and how much he knew about baseball, he had a memory that wandered. He wasn't on top of everything the way McCarthy was. If Bill needed a pitcher late in the game, he would often forget to have somebody warming up.

MacPhail hired Bucky Harris to be the manager in 1947. I think Bucky got a raw deal. He could have had that big Yankee dynasty that Stengel inherited. In 1948, we had a chance to win the pennant, but we lost it on the last day of the season.

Bucky was a great manager, a great guy, a lot like McCarthy. He was the same way when he was a player. Bucky was tough as nails. He'd fight anybody. Unlike McCarthy, Bucky had played many years in the big leagues. He was a psychologist. He treated every ballplayer differently.

Bucky was MacPhail's man, and after MacPhail left, George Weiss was the one who fired him. And Weiss brought in Stengel, who was regarded as a nice man but a clown. He had never won anything with Brooklyn or Boston. He inherited this great team with young players coming up. You and I could have managed the team and gone away for the summer.

Casey came in during spring training in 1949, and I'll never forget the first meeting we had.

"I know nothing about the American League," Casey said. "You are all big league ballplayers. I won't give you any signs. You're on your own. You play. This is my year just to observe. I will find out what the American League is all about."

And that's exactly what happened. I tell you, it was an exciting year. We had some characters on that '49 team. Frank Shea was unbelievably funny. He was the first one to come in with those rubber masks, an ape like Frankenstein. When you leave the stadium, all these kids want autographs, and Shea made up a cast, and he'd tell the kids, "I can't sign. I broke my arm." He put ketchup on it. Frank was real clever. He was a great pitcher, and it's a shame he hurt his arm.

John Lindell was another. Are you kidding? Lindell was hung bigger than anybody. He used to take that thing and whack me on the back of the neck with it. He would pee on me in the shower. Tommy Henrich was pretty good, too. He wouldn't start anything, but if Page or Stirnweiss had an idea, he'd go along. Joe Page was the biggest liar you'd ever want to meet. You knew he was lying. He'd still tell it.

I was never an innovator. I was the guy they pulled all the jokes on. They nailed my shoes to the floor. Oh yeah, my spiked shoes. I'd go to put them on . . .

Joe Page, Stirnweiss, and I bought a hunting camp in Presque Isle, Maine. I don't know why I went in on it because I didn't hunt. We all had shares in it. Joe would go up there more than anybody. He'd bring his friends, and they played poker. And then when Joe needed some money, he sold the cabin. He didn't tell us about it. And I still hadn't been there.

I played every game in '49. I didn't get hurt. Tommy Henrich counted up the injuries. He was in the hospital, and was very nice to me, saying the only player the Yankees couldn't afford to lose was Rizzuto. And that year, Joe DiMaggio was hurt much of the season. He never discussed it with anybody, but I knew about it. Joe just took things as they came. He was like Yogi. Joe had married Dorothy Arnold in '42, and by the time he got out of the army they got divorced. They almost got together again. See, in those days Joe was tough to live with. They said he was an introvert. All he wanted to do was

Joe DiMaggio. Author collection

to go to Toot Shor's and sit in the corner and talk baseball. Dorothy was beautiful, and I guess she wanted to go out and be seen. And Joe was very moody. *Very* moody. You could go a week without talking to him. He wouldn't talk. He'd sulk. That's pretty tough when you have to live with someone like that.

It was a bad time for him emotionally because when you don't talk about it, keep it inside you, it's ten times as bad.

And yet Joe and Joe Page were friends. Page loved him. Everybody did. They knew Joe was putting money in their pockets. Joe was a complete ballplayer. He was all business on the field.

There was a mystery about Joe. You never knew what Joe was thinking or doing. Just watching him play every day was a thrill.

See, Joe D always needed somebody—I don't know if you'd call him a flunky. "Go get me a pack of cigarettes."

"Go to the movies with me."

Or, "Let's go here."

Joe always had somebody like a caddy. Lefty Gomez was the best he ever had because Lefty wouldn't take any guff from him, but Lefty would do a lot of things for Joe.

In '49, Joe came back for a great series against the Red Sox. The Sox came to town with a one-game lead with two games to play. They had a big lead in that first game. They were beating us 4–0. Birdie Tebbetts, the Red Sox catcher, was popping off during my second at bat.

"Tomorrow we're going to pitch Quinn," the big bonus kid from Yale. And Birdie bragged they were going to drink the champagne. I went back and told everyone in the clubhouse what he said, and boy, they were mad.

We ended up winning 5–4, and the next day we won 5–3 and won the pennant and the World Series. Joe Page, who was as good a pitcher as anybody, pitched 6 2/3 innings of one-hit ball to assure the victory. For three years, he was as good as anybody I ever saw in my life. When you saw him hop the fence in right field the way he did, and walk in, you knew he was going to get them out. He'd fire the ball. Page was really something. He was really great.

During that two-game series against the Red Sox, Johnny Pesky knocked me down, rolled over me, and spiked me. Pesky had a way of sliding that got him in a lot of fights. And that got the Yankees really riled up.

The same thing happened in the '49 World Series when Jackie Robinson hit me and knocked me out. He came into second base, started to slide as I was coming across the bag, and at the last second he changed his mind, and he was so quick that he came in and hit me with his shoulder as I threw the ball, and we got a double play, but I went over his head and landed on my head, and I was knocked out. And when I came to, I saw the whole Yankee team—DiMaggio, Henrich, Keller, all of them.

About two innings later, Robinson doubled, and as he stood on second base, he apologized. He told me what had happened, that he had started his slide and then changed his mind.

"I didn't mean to do it," he said, but he said he needed to leave the field as soon as he could because he knew how mad the Yankee players would be.

He apologized, and I accepted it.

But Pesky, he did it on purpose. He did it every time. He made a rolling block coming in. He'd roll and hit you and then roll over you, and then he'd stomp on you.

As I said, in 1949 Casey pretty much left us alone, and then in 1950 and 1951 he started that platooning system. I wasn't platooned. In 1950, I won the Most Valuable Player Award, but then after DiMaggio left after the 1951 season, I was the last of the old guard left. Tommy Henrich was gone. Charlie Keller was gone. Bill Dickey was gone. Everybody. Casey wanted all of the old-timers out so he could get all the young kids so he could let them know who was boss.

Casey and DiMaggio never got along. Joe would say, "How can this guy win?" But we won because we had talent. I was the last of the old guard, and I kept playing—in 1951, 1952, 1953, but then he started platooning me. We never hit it off after that, and then there was the day in 1956 he called me in and told me I was going to be released.

It was Old-Timers' Day, and that was one of the worst days of my life. Stengel called me in, him and George Weiss. The old-timers were out there, and we were taking pictures. I didn't know that I would become an old-timer in about a half hour.

They told me Irv Noren was hurt, and they needed another outfielder, another left-handed hitter for the World Series.

He said, "We want you to go over this list with us to see who is the most logical player to go."

"Charlie Silvera," I said.

Yogi was catching. They said no. I mentioned a couple of fringe pitchers, and every time I'd say a name, they'd say no, until I started to get the hint. When they said, "Let's go over the list again," it started to dawn on me.

They finally got up enough nerve to say, "Phil, we'd like to give you your release. And tomorrow you can come back again. You won't be eligible for the World Series, but you'll get your full World Series share and you can finish the year with us. Next year, if you want to come to spring training, you can."

I was really crushed. I got dressed. George Stirnweiss saved the day, maybe saved my life. I might have jumped off the George Washington Bridge. A ballplayer who hasn't made plans for the future thinks he's going to go on playing indefinitely. Suddenly, you're without a job, and you hadn't gone to college, and what the hell am I going to do?

George, who had been released several years before this, was at the game, and he was outside the clubhouse door when I came out. There were tears in my eyes, and he asked me what happened, and I told him.

He drove all the way home with me, told me his feelings and what had happened to him, when he took the train home after he was let go.

George really helped me. He got me over that rough spot, and fortunately I didn't blast anybody—the Yankees had done a lot for me—and as a result I got television appearances. And I did a lot of other shows because they all felt sorry for me and felt the Yankees had done me wrong. I got a great deal of sympathy, and then I got to do some broadcasting—I did some New York Giants games at the end of the year. In fact, the Giants wanted to sign me as an announcer, but they were moving to San Francisco the next year, and I would have had to move.

I said no, and then Baltimore wanted to sign me, but I would have had to move to Baltimore. It was a year-round job. I had to do public relations work in the winter. And in December the Yankees asked me, and everything fell right into place.

• *12* •

Ron Santo

John Holland was like a father. He made a lot of sense. I was emotional, but when he said, "You'll be back," I knew he meant it.

—Ron Santo

$\mathscr{R}$on Santo was born on February 25, 1940, in Seattle, Washington. A nine-time All-Star, Santo played third base for the Chicago Cubs for fourteen years. He starred from 1960 until 1973, and he played one additional season for the Chicago White Sox. During our discussion, it was clear to me that for him the most interesting part of his career was the story of how, despite missteps by Cubs minor league decision makers, he made it to start for the Cubs at age twenty. Santo was a man of deep emotion, as you will read. He was elected posthumously to the baseball Hall of Fame in 2012.

I met him at the Cubs Fantasy Camp in Mesa in 1994, and over lunch I happened to mention I had done a book with Yankee manager Billy Martin. He reached across the table and lunged for me, before apologizing for losing his temper. I was never sure why, but he hated Martin, and he was reacting to hearing his name.

Santo was a Cubs broadcaster from 1990 until he death on December 3, 2010. Santo had suffered from diabetes since he was a teenager, a disease he first revealed in 1971. He started a foundation that raised more than $65 million for diabetes research.

Ron Santo: I was exceptional. I made the freshman baseball team at Franklin High School (in Seattle) when you were not allowed to make the team as a freshman. I played third base, and I played all through my high school career

Ron Santo. Photofest

until my senior year, when our catcher got hurt. I went behind the plate because I had a good arm.

I didn't know it, but a lot of scouts were scouting me. I was contacted one day my sophomore year by Dave Tacher, a bird-dog scout for the Chicago Cubs. He walked up to me. I didn't know who he was. He didn't talk about signing me or anything like that. Dave was a spastic, and so he walked funny, and he talked funny, but I could understand him. He told me he was a friend of Rogers Hornsby and when they met he was in a wheelchair.

"Rogers convinced me I could get out of the wheelchair," Dave said.

Dave and I became close friends.

My senior year, I won the first all-star award. In the state of Washington, they played an all-star game with sixty players from the state. You played three innings, and after the game two players were chosen to play in a game between the New York all-stars and the United States all-stars. Two players were chosen from each state, and I was chosen from the state of Washington.

It took fourteen hours to fly to New York City one way. The DC-6 went up and down, and up and down, and that was something because I had never in my life been out of Seattle. I was eighteen years old.

I worked out, and I started as a catcher. Joe Torre, who was from Brooklyn, was the third baseman for the New York All-Stars. The New York All-Stars beat us 9–0. They had a pitcher—I don't remember his name—who was about six-foot-six, and he could throw ninety plus. He only allowed two hits, and I had both of them. I didn't do a good job defensively, but the scouts knew I had a good arm, but my heart was not in catching. My heart was at third base.

A lot of scouts were at the game, and I was awarded player of the game. The Yankees scout asked if I would stay in New York and work out with the Yankees.

"No," I said, "I want to go back home."

It was the first time I had been away from home, and I had been away a week. The Yankee scout said he would come to Seattle and sit down with my dad—he was really my stepfather. My real dad had left us when I was five years old, and I never saw him again until he showed up when I was nineteen and in pro ball.

When I got home, I started to get phone calls. My dad set up meetings with all sixteen major league clubs.

We lived in a duplex in Garland Village. We didn't have a lot monetarily, but love-wise it was wonderful. I had a lot of confidence in my stepfather. I loved him very much. He came into my life when I was twelve years old.

The first scout who walked in was from the Cleveland Indians. It was very quick. He said to my dad, "We're very interested in your son. We'll give him $50,000 to sign."

When he said fifty thousand dollars, my dad and I looked at each other, and all of a sudden I couldn't swallow.

Right away my dad said, "Where will he be playing?" My dad also told him we were going to talk to all the scouts.

I hadn't made up my mind about a team. I was more of a National League fan, though. I would watch the Game of the Week on Saturdays and Sundays. Saturday was National League. Sunday was American League, and I missed a lot of Sundays. I never missed a Saturday. The Brooklyn Dodgers and the New York Yankees were my favorite teams, and of course I loved Mickey Mantle. But it wasn't like I was crazy about them.

The Indians scout said, "You'll go to Double A ball, and we'll give you five hundred a month. We know you're seeing other scouts. Let us know. We'd really love to have ya."

The next hour another scout came, and every team made an offer of $50,000 or more. The highest offer came from the Cincinnati Reds. I lived in Seattle, and I had worked at Seattle Stadium since I was a freshman in high school. I worked in the press box, and then became a bat boy, worked as an usher, and then my senior year I worked in the clubhouse. I shined Vada Pinson's shoes before he went to the big leagues.

Freddie Hutchinson was the Seattle manager. A most wonderful man for a young kid. I highly respected him because he was a guy who was tough, but tough in a different way. When Fred said something, he meant it. You had to respect what he said. He was a calm person, but you could see in his face when he was upset about something. He had nothing but respect. He'd fight for you. You knew he would. I would see how much the players respected this man.

Fred had seen me play when I was young. My freshman year I couldn't hit it out of the ballpark, but I could one-hop the wall. I was only five-two my freshman year. My sophomore year I went to five-eight, and by senior year I was six feet.

Cincinnati came to Seattle to play an exhibition game. I went out to take batting practice. I weighed 165 pounds and I had my 31-ounce, 34-inch bat. Don Newcombe was throwing batting practice. He threw ninety plus. His first pitch was a fastball inside. I didn't care how fast he threw. I had a gift. I had a quick bat.

The ball ran in and busted my bat. First pitch. And it was the only bat I had. Ed Bailey, a catcher on the Reds, threw a bat to me.

"Here kid, try this one," he said. The bat had to be 38 ounces and thick. I was too embarrassed to say, "I can't use this one." What could I do? I'll be honest with you. I didn't hit the ball well. I didn't show anything. I looked like a piece of shit.

I thought I had ruined my chances with Cincinnati. Later, Dewey Soriano, the Seattle general manager, came to my house with a scout. I had told my dad, "I don't think they're interested." I introduced Dewey to my dad, and Dewey said, "Your son has been a great employee at the ballpark and a wonderful kid."

"We're very impressed," the scout said to me. "We know you can play third base." That was very important to me. "But we also know you can catch. And more catchers are needed in the big leagues than third basemen. Here's what we are offering. We are offering you $80,000 to sign and a Double A contract. We would like you to start off in Seattle with the Triple A club. But we will give you a Double A contract. We don't want to rush you, but we feel your being a hometown boy, we feel you can play there."

"I'd rather not play in my hometown," I said. "I'd rather go to Double A."

Because playing at home is *a lot* of pressure.

They left, and other teams came and made offers, but I had still not heard from the Chicago Cubs. I used to watch the Cubs on national TV. Ernie Banks was someone I just idolized. I thought he was an outstanding hitter and person. But I always felt sorry for the Cubs. Because they weren't a winner. I don't know—I was always for the underdog, especially the Cubs. I always wanted them to win.

I was surprised I hadn't heard from Dave Tacher in two days.

I loved Dave. He had so much confidence in me. My sophomore year he had told me, "You're going to play in the major leagues as a third baseman."

Dave knew talent. He knew the game of baseball.

The next morning, I got a call from Dave. He was calling from Chicago. He slurred his speech when he talked. It was almost as though he was crying all the time.

"Ronnie," he said. "I know all the scouts. I know all your deals. Ron, the reason I haven't come over, all they are going to offer you is $20,000 and a Double A contract at $500 a month.

"Dave, tell them to come over anyway," I said.

Dave flew in, and my dad and I met him and head scout [Roy] Hardrock Johnson. I don't know his first name.

Hardrock Johnson said, "We're offering you $20,000, and we want you as a catcher, because we don't think you can play third base in the majors."

He had never even seen me play. That bothered me because Dave told me I'd be a third baseman.

"That's the deal," he said. "Take it or leave it."

I would have told him to get out, but my dad handled it very well. He didn't have a temper even though he was Italian.

"Thank you very much, Mr. Johnson," he said.

Dad was upset, and so was I. Cause Johnson had no respect. He had driven Dave because Dave didn't drive.

I said to Dave, "You stay. I will drive you home."

Dave couldn't apologize more.

"Oh Ron," he said, "How could he say those things to you?"

"Dave," I said, "if I sign with the Cubs it will be because of you. I'm going to sit with my dad tonight. We're going to go over everything, and I'll call you first thing in the morning. You're not out of the picture."

That evening, I sat down with my dad. We talked about everything. We talked about money. My dad couldn't believe the money I was offered.

"It'll set you up for life," he said. Then he said, "I want you to know something. I believe very strongly that you can play in the big leagues, and I believe you will get there. It's a matter of asking, Where will you get lost? How many years will you have to spend in the minor leagues? Why don't you look at it this way: Do you want to take the money? You can put the money in the bank. If you take Cincinnati and you don't make it, you'll have money in the bank. It'll give you a start. Does the money matter? What do you want to do?"

"No, dad, it really doesn't," I said.

"Then it's up to you," he said. I'll tell you one thing: Dave Tacher has as much confidence in you as I do. Think about that. Sleep on it."

The next morning, I woke up. I had no doubt in my mind. I was going with the Cubs.

I signed, and I spent exactly one year and two months in the minor leagues. How many players only spend one year in the minor leagues?

The February after I signed, I went to a three-week camp in Mesa, Arizona, with all the top prospects. Rogers Hornsby was the batting instructor and one of the Cubs coaches. He was the key man for hitting.

There were thirty of us, and we slept in barracks. I went there as a catcher, but the Cubs had five catchers, good catchers like Moe Thacker, and Sammy Taylor, but not good hitters.

There were higher bonus babies than me. I was not considered a high bonus baby. We had intersquad games. We hit, and on the second day Rogers Hornsby said to me, "Ron, I wouldn't change anything with you. The only thing I'd suggest, move back and away from

Rogers Hornsby. Author collection

the plate a little bit. It'll give you better perspective on the curveball."

I did that, and I felt comfortable. And I was a pull hitter. You don't learn to go the other way unless you're a singles hitter. Not that I was a home run hitter. I didn't know if I was. I hit line drives, and a few of them went a long way. On those fields, they didn't have fences, so I had to run around the bases.

A week went by, and I wasn't playing. Elvin Tappe, the manager, was using his bonus-baby catchers. All I was doing was catching batting practice, picking up the equipment, and not getting an opportunity.

I walked up to Elvin Tappe, and I said, "Mr. Tappe, am I going to get an opportunity to play?"

"Who do you think you are?" he said. He never cussed. But it was, "I'll tell you when you play."

I didn't like the way he did that. Even though I was young, only eighteen, I said, "I don't think I'm anybody, but I've been here a week, and I haven't played. How do you know how good I am?"

"You sit until I tell you," Tappe said. "You pick up the equipment until I tell you."

I just walked away.

That day—a Saturday—one of the catchers got hurt. I was sitting in the dugout and Tappe said to me, "Get the equipment on. You're in."

My first time at the plate, I hit a line drive over the left field wall. Aw God, I can't tell you what that felt like. I'm a line drive hitter, but I didn't expect a home run. The next time up, I hit a line drive down the left field line for a double. Those were my only two at bats.

The next day, I was starting, and I played every day. I hit four home runs that week.

At the end of the three weeks, Rogers Hornsby took twenty of us over to the bleachers. I was sitting in the second row with Billy Williams. Billy and I became friends. It was funny how we hit it off. I saw the talent with his bat. The guy was exceptional. And a wonderful person. There were maybe three blacks on the ball club, all wonderful guys, and all had talent. Billy was exceptional.

Rogers Hornsby goes down the first row. He said to the first guy, "You might as well go home. You won't get past A ball." He went to the next guy. "You won't get past A ball." The next guy. "You won't get past C ball." I was listening to this imagining that if he said to me, "You might as well go home," I would feel I had no chance.

Hornsby said the same thing to the first guy in our row. To Billy, he said, "You will play in the big leagues, and you can play now." And he says to me, "You can hit in the big leagues right now." And to the rest of the prospects he said, "You'll never get past A ball."

Billy Williams and I were the only two who made it to the big leagues.

[Santo spent 1959 with San Antonio in Double A ball. He hit .327 with 11 home runs and 87 runs batted in in 136 games.]

I went to spring training with the Cubs in 1960. I got a chance to play. I got hot and played in a lot of the exhibition games. Our manager was Charlie Grimm, a funny man who let you play the game. He was a good guy to be around. I was a nonroster player but I felt strongly I was going to make the team. In my mind, I was thinking I was not going to the minor leagues.

There was one week left in spring training. The Dodgers were coming into town the weekend before we were to break camp. Charlie called me into his office. He said, "Ron, you have two good days here against the Dodgers, and you will break camp with the Cubs. You'll be our third baseman."

You'd think that that was pressure, but it wasn't. I was hot. I was having a good spring. We faced Stan Williams and Don Drysdale. The first time up, I hit a home run off Williams. I had another base hit, so I was two for four. And I made some plays.

I didn't know Stan Williams. Drysdale was more intimidating. I used to watch Drysdale on TV. Once when Drysdale was facing Henry Aaron, I said to my mother, "God must have given them a special gift."

I never imagined myself facing Don Drysdale. He threw inside, threw ninety plus, and he was mean. You heard so much about what a competitor he was. I was intimidated, but I hung in there.

Against Drysdale, I went two for four.

Grimm called me in, and he says, "You're breaking camp."

I was housed in the minor league facility, and he told me to move into the Miracle Inn. I got a room, and I called my wife and I told her I was going to the big leagues.

I hadn't signed a contract yet. I haven't even met John Holland, the general manager. But I was going to.

At seven o'clock that evening, the phone rang.

"Ron, this is John Holland. Would you meet me in Charlie Grimm's room?"

"Sure, I'll be right down."

I was thinking, *I'm going to sign a major league contract.*

I walked in the door. You know when you walk into a room and you know something is wrong? I was nineteen. Charlie sat down. John Holland was already sitting down. I was standing, and John said, "Son, sit down."

"I don't want to sit down," I said.

"Would you please sit down?"

"No, I don't want to. Something's wrong."

"Okay, son," said Holland, "here's what happened. We just made a trade. We traded Ron Perranoski, Johnny Goryl, and Lee Handley to the Dodgers for third baseman Don Zimmer. Charlie and I talked about this, and we feel you're a little too young. We need a veteran guy for third base."

I'm choked. I'm emotional. I'm not yelling. I feel like I'm going to cry. But I held it in. I turned to Charlie.

"Charlie, you promised me. You told me I'd break camp and be your third baseman."

I said to John, "I know I can play. I'm not too young. I've proven it this spring. I am not going to the minor leagues. I am going home."

"Wait a minute," they said.

"No," I said.

Because I was going to start crying, I walked out the door. I went down to my room and bawled like a baby.

I waited until I could speak and relax a little bit, and I called my wife.

"I'm coming home," I told her. "I'm quitting baseball. They lied to me."

"No, no, Ron, you shouldn't do that," she said.

"I can't help it," I said. "I earned this job. I deserved this job. I know I can play here. I'm coming home."

"Well, do what you feel you have to do," she said.

There was a knock on the door. It was John Holland. He came into my room.

"Son," he said, "I know you're upset. We know you can play in the big leagues. We know you're going to be here. We just made a move, and we have to send you to Triple A ball, but you'll be back. We're going to give you a major league contract."

"I don't care about the money, John. I want to play in the big leagues."

"No," he said, "we're going to give you major league money to play in Triple A ball because we know you'll be coming up to the big leagues."

"I don't want it. I'm going home."

"Now settle down, son."

John Holland was like a father. He made a lot of sense. I was emotional, but when he said, "You'll be back," I knew he meant it. So, I signed and went to Triple A ball with Houston.

My heart wasn't in it. I got off to a terrible start. My manager was Enos Slaughter, a wonderful man. He loved to fight, and I was in that kind of a mood. He used to start things and tell us to go out there and mix it up. Enos was very aggressive. He was all speed because he had that speed. He loved guys to go the other way. He loved guys who wouldn't take any shit. And I was in one of those moods all the time. I was always getting hot. I wouldn't start a fight, but I would never back down from one. He loved that. He'd be right in it. He just loved it.

Anyway, we started at the end of April, and I got off to a terrible start. Every day, I watched in the paper to see how the Cubs were doing. They weren't doing too well. I'd say to myself, *Maybe they will bring you up. Naaah. I doubt it. I'll probably be here all year.* So, I really didn't get my stuff together.

Then Slaughter said to me, "I hear John Holland is coming down here."

It was the second week in June. I was hitting around .260 and didn't have many home runs. I figured I should pick up the tempo, and I got hot. John came in and watched me for about a week, and then I got a call at 8:30 in the morning on June 15.

"Head to Pittsburgh tonight."

I started for the Cubs the next day.

Charlie Grimm was no longer manager. He went to the broadcasting booth. Lou Boudreau took over, and Lou started me, hit me sixth, and he had a lot of confidence in me. He knew I could play. We were on a nine-game losing streak, and in a doubleheader against the Pirates, I faced Bob Friend and Vern Law.

It was the first day I was with the Cubs. I was sitting on the bench, and Ernie Banks said to me in a joyful way, "Are you nervous?"

"Oh boy, am I nervous," I said.

"Well, look kid," Ernie said, "think of Bob Friend and Vern Law as minor league pitchers when you go to the plate.

It was a great thought, though I knew it was Bob Friend and Vern Law. But that's the kind of person Ernie always was. I only saw Ernie get mad once in my thirteen years with him. Jack Sanford hit him for the twelfth time. Because Ernie used to nail Sanford. In those days, you could do that.

Ron Santo. National Baseball Hall of Fame

Ernie Banks was tremendous with me. He was the only one. In spring training, I wasn't on the roster, but I was still eating with the veterans, having breakfast with them, and nobody would sit with me. Nobody. Because you were taking somebody's job. The only guy who would talk to me was Ernie Banks.

And yet you could not sit down and have a real serious conversation with Ernie Banks. Not something that was bothering you. My second year I hit behind Banks, and he hit forty-two home runs, and I got thrown at forty-two times. I'd say to him, "Because of your home runs, I'm spending a lot of time in the dirt." He just laughed. That's the way it was. You accepted it. This was all respect.

The Pirates would win the World Series that year, but against Friend and Law that day I went 4–7 and drove in five runs, and we won both games. That's how I broke into the big leagues.

Lou Boudreau was a fine, fine manager. One time he fined me $50, which was a lot of money, because I didn't slide. He was manager and third base coach. I was coming into third, and he was laying on his stomach, and I came in standing up and got thrown out, and he called a meeting the next day and in front of everybody he said, "Young fella, you're fined $50 for not sliding." From then on, I was going to slide into first, second, third, and home. You know what I mean?

Mr. Wrigley didn't believe in two-year contracts, so that's when Lou went back to the broadcast booth, and they came up with the College of Coaches—the rotating coaches. Being as young as I was, my only concern was staying in the big leagues. As a rookie, you don't look at your ball club. You don't realize you're not winning. After you establish yourself, that's when you say to yourself, *We don't have enough talent. This is bad.*

You had to prove yourself to the veterans. You also took a lot of razzing from the other teams, especially from the catchers. But I was oblivious to that, too. All I cared about was making contact, doing my job.

I felt I had a gift. As a diabetic, I had to go through a lot, but it was easy to play the game and to get better. I loved working. I had great work habits. Facing a pitcher from sixty feet, six inches away wasn't difficult. You had your bad days, but you knew you'd bounce back. I knew I was good, and then all of a sudden I could see myself getting respect.

When I came to the Cubs, Don Zimmer played third. Jerry Kindall was the second baseman, and then Zimmer moved to second, and Jerry and him were back and forth, and I played third. We had this revolving coaching system and Zim went on the radio with Lou Boudreau. Zim was always so interesting. I loved to talk to him about the game. He would talk about the strategy of the game. I learned a lot by listening to him.

I was in the clubhouse listening, and Zim said, "This coaching system is killing one of our best prospects, Ron Santo."

Meaning every two weeks you have a new guy coming in to manage and telling me what to do, where to play, and the next guy would tell me something different. Zim felt the system was ruining a lot of young players such as Lou Brock. Because of that, Zimmer was let go. He was released. After I heard him on the radio, he was gone.

In 1962, my teammate was Ken Hubbs. Kenny was about six-foot-three. He was a great basketball player. He could stuff the ball. He was very talented. He fielded like a gazelle. Kenny was a deeply religious Mormon. He never swore, never drank.

You knew he was going to do something great, and in 1962 he was the National League Rookie of the Year. We would sit together on the DC-6 charter and he was always scared to fly. He wanted me to save a seat for him.

The following year we were roommates in spring training. Every night, I would come in early because I was working really hard, and every night he would come in at around ten o'clock.

"What do you have going on out there, big boy?" I asked him.

"I have a surprise for you," he said.

"What is it?"

"I can't tell you until spring training is over."

At the end of spring training, we got on a plane to Chicago. He seemed more relaxed than usual.

"I want to show you something," he said. He pulled out his wallet and showed me his pilot's license. He was taking flying lessons after every game, and he got in enough hours to get his license.

"When I get up there," Kenny said to me, "when I fly, it's like being next to God."

That helped his fear of flying. Kenny was from Colton, California. He met a girl he was going to marry, and I was going to be his best man. The ceremony was going to be in February. He then decided not to marry her because the family didn't think she was a devout enough Mormon. That was hard. And that's when he ended up buying a plane.

After he separated from her, he needed to occupy his mind, so in Colton he bought a Cessna 180. At the end of 1963, I flew with him just before I

Ken Hubbs's funeral. Author collection

headed home to Seattle. I was a nervous wreck. Ken didn't do instrument fly-ing. It was a beautiful day, and he could phone all the way to his house. His dad was in a wheelchair. He had twin younger brothers. Ken was his dad's legs.

We flew around, landed, and had dinner.

"I'm going to Salt Lake City to pick up my best buddy who has just got-ten married," he told me. "I'm going to fly him back to Colton. We'll spend a couple days, and I'll fly him back."

I went to the airport and headed to Seattle. I was home, and the next day I was in my mother's car when I heard it on the radio: Ken Hubbs is missing. By the time I got home, they had found him.

His dad told me it was a nice day when he went to the airport. He flew to Salt Lake City and picked up his buddy. He took off to return to Colton, and twenty minutes after he took off his friend's wife called to tell them they had forgotten something. When the guy in the tower called to tell him, Kenny radioed back, "I have run into a front. I need a flight pattern. I don't know where I am."

He didn't know where the horizon was. The last person to see him was riding in a train. He saw Kenny's plane crash headlong into a sheet of ice on a lake, and they were both killed.

I went to the funeral and stayed with his folks. The whole town of Colton shut down. It was hard to believe. Kenny was twenty-three years old.

· 13 ·

Ellis Clary

I'm so glad I got over there with them bastards. Nobody else had
a collection of goofs like we had.

—Ellis Clary

$\mathcal{E}$llis Clary was born on September
11, 1914, in Valdosta, Georgia. He
began his career during World War
II playing with the Washington Senators, then in 1943 was traded to the
lowly St. Louis Browns. Clary, a utility infielder, didn't play much with
the Browns, but he had a ringside seat
to the only World Series the Browns
were ever in, and the next year he had
a dugout seat as the Browns installed
one-armed outfielder Pete Gray in
centerfield as a way to bolster atten-
dance. Unfortunately, Gray's presence
caused tremendous resentment among
the veteran Browns players and cost
the Browns any chances of winning
their second consecutive pennant.
Clary watched it all unfold. He then
went on to play eight more years in

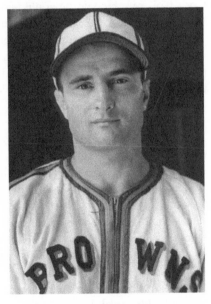

Ellis Clary. Author collection

the minor leagues, after which he was a coach for Washington, then scouted
for the Minnesota Twins for twenty-four years after the Senators moved to
Minneapolis–St. Paul. He later worked as a scout for both the Chicago White

Sox and Toronto Blue Jays, retiring in 1993. Clary died on June 2, 2000, in Valdosta at the age of eighty-five.

Ellis Clary: I started playing in Valdosta when I was a boy. We played on the sandlots every day. In the winter if it was cold, we'd play football in the morning and baseball in the afternoon when it was a little warmer. Yeah, we played something every day that we could.

When I was eighteen, I played in the summertime on a semipro team in a place called Vienna, Georgia. We played every day but Sunday. Along came a scout who signed me to the Birmingham team in the Southern League. Birmingham was independent. Back then, they didn't have the farm system they have today. Most of the Southern League teams were independent.

Clyde Milan was our manager. Clyde played for Washington, and he was a superman. Everyone loved Clyde Milan. He died on Tinker Field in Orlando during spring training when he was a coach.

I got into the Washington chain the second year. Early Wynn was on that team. He was seventeen years old. Early went to a ballpark in Florida for a tryout. He was barefooted with a T-shirt and a pair of blue jeans on and a Coca-Cola cap. He said he could play.

"We'll find out," they said. And he wound up in the Hall of Fame. Things like that don't happen anymore.

My manager in the minors was Wilbur Bill "Raw Meat" Rogers, the greatest human being that you could ever imagine. Me and Wynn roomed together on three teams, and as I told Early many times, "If it hadn't been for Raw Meat Rogers, we'd a never gotten out of the Florida State League."

"That's right," Early said.

We were horseshit, but in a word Rogers bullshitted us into thinking we could play. He was the best man in the world for a young player to ever be with. We were terrible, but he just put up with it and kept sticking with us. Wynn had a good arm, but he couldn't throw a strike. I was horseshit. And he stuck with us.

I could run fast. I led the league in stolen bases. Red Meat let me run when I wanted to. In one game, I stole second on the first pitch, stole third on the next pitch, and Red Meat just yelled out, "Hell, go on home." And on the next pitch, I stole home.

In 1938, I was on the Charlotte baseball team, and once I beat Jesse Owens in the fifty-yard dash in Richmond, Virginia, but it didn't count because we were racing one hundred yards. At halfway, I stood ahead of him. Of course, I jumped the gun and ran into the lead. I thought I had Owens beat. I stayed ahead of him as far as about the fifty-yard line. I was envisioning getting a telegram from Adolf Hitler for beating Jesse Owens. But you could not beat that fella. You could *not* beat him.

I played with Washington in 1942, and then in 1943 I was traded to the St. Louis Browns in the middle of the summer. [He was traded with Ox Miller to the Browns for Harlond Clift and Johnny Niggeling.] I felt like committing suicide, but it's the funniest thing that happened to me because you never know what's around the corner. I felt terrible, I mean bad. And then I got over with them clowns, and it was the greatest group of all time. And the thing that we did—we won the pennant and got into the World Series. And the fun we had. And the characters on that team—there will never be an assemblage like that again.

I was upset until I met those meatheads over there. A month before I got traded, Washington had a little scuffle with the Browns. Somebody in front of me hit a home run, and the next pitch went up behind my head. Back then, you wore a cloth cap and not a helmet.

"Well," I said, "I'll get that son of a bitch," and I bunted, and Denny Galehouse covered it, and even though I made the third out, I slammed into him and knocked him out into right field.

When I was traded to the Browns, I was scared to go into their clubhouse. The dressing room in St. Louis was upstairs, and I walked in and looked around, and Rick Ferrell, who was catching for the Browns, spotted me, and Rick came to the door and shook my hand, and he said, "Welcome to our nine." This is exactly what he said, and I told him many times that was one of the greatest things, and he became a good friend of mine. Rick was a fine man.

In 1944, the Browns held our spring training in Cape Girardeau in Missouri. We didn't go to Florida because of the war. The cold wasn't bad. There was a lake near the ballpark, and Sig Jakucki and Tex Shirley would go out to the lake where ducks lived, and they would go and gather up four or five or six duck eggs, and they'd slip one of the duck eggs into the pocket of a teammate, and when he'd sit down he'd make the biggest mess you've ever seen. Jesus Christ, it looked like he had had a bowel movement.

These guys would make up some shit all the time. Jakucki and Shirley were two of our pitchers, and the two of them could tear up a bar. Jakucki was in the army. I don't know which branch. We were playing in New York, and Jakucki would live in the Traveler's Bar, which was across the street from the hotel where we stayed. Some fool came in there and sat next to him, and they started jawing, and this guy pulled out a gun. Jakucki knocked the guy flat on his back, threw the gun by his side, and walked out.

After Jakucki pitched a game, he would disappear, and you might not see him for two or three days. When he'd pitch in St. Louis, he'd take a shower, and ten minutes after the game Jakucki would be heading out to work them bars. George McQuinn, our first baseman, was always one of the last to leave, and McQuinn would say to him, "See you Monday."

And Jakucki would say to him, "See ya Thursday."

He'd laugh and take off.

When we went to Cape Girardeau, Jakucki and Tex Shirley had never seen each other before. The first night, the whole club is in the bar. Cape Girardeau is not a very big town. It was the only bar, and so the whole team was in there drinking. Tex got up and went to get his beer, and everybody was half in the bag, and when he came back Tex decided he would pour a little beer over Jakucki's head. He'd give him a shampoo. As he walked by, he poured beer on Jakucki's head, and Sig got up and hit Shirley right in the mouth and damn near knocked the wall over with him. The next morning, Tex's mouth looked like a freight train had run through it. He had it all taped up. He told our manager Luke Sewell he was riding and a horse threw him against a fence.

After that, Sig and Tex tolerated each other.

One night in Philadelphia, the two of them tore up a barroom. They turned over the tables, busted a door. The restroom was up a flight of stairs, in the mezzanine. The two of them got in a fight with someone in the men's room, and the guy flew over the balcony, and it was a big mess.

But that was very common with them guys.

When the 1944 season started, we had four good pitchers. They were like the pitchers in Atlanta today. [Greg Maddux, John Smoltz, Tom Glavine, Steve Avery.] We had Jack Kramer [17–13], Nelson Potter [19–7], Denny Galehouse [9–10], and Bob Muncrief [13–8]. Those four bastards, when they went out there, you figured you could win the game. Jakucki [13–9], Sam Zoldak [0–0] and Al Hollingsworth [6–7] were the second liners, and we had George Caster [6–6], our relief man, and Tex Shirley [5–4]. But it was the Big Four—they could beat anybody—that's what won it for us.

We started the season winning nine straight games. Everybody was running their goddamn mouth. I remember telling them, "If we go undefeated, we may get to the Rose Bowl or the Sugar Bowl."

Vern Stephens was our star shortstop [Stephens led the league in RBIs with 109 and was second in the league with 20 homers], and we had George McQuinn [72 RBIs] at first base, the best fielder in baseball, and Al Zarilla, who was coming along, had a big year [.299 batting average]. That was a pretty good team.

I had to room with Vern Stephens one year on the road. No one could put up with that shit. His bed wouldn't be touched. Any gal who looked at him would hop into bed with him. They'd call his hotel room, and I'd answer to three names: Vern, Stevie, and Junior.

"Is Vern there?" "Is Stevie there?" "Is Junior there?"

One day in Philadelphia, Vern came out to Shibe Park. His locker was right next to mine. This was when I was rooming with him. He came up to

Vern Stephens. Author collection

me, and he said, "Roomie, I don't think I can make it today. I ain't touched a bed all night. I haven't been to sleep."

This was a day game. Big, tall Russ Christopher, a side-armer, was going to pitch for the A's. Even though Vern didn't think he'd make it, he went out there and Christopher struck him out three times, and he didn't even foul one off. The fourth time he got up in the ninth inning, and Stevie hit the roof of the upper deck, and it bounced back into the ball field. It hit the fascia and came back, and we won the game. Now ain't that something? Finally he made a connection and hit a rocket out of there.

Vern was a better-than-average shortstop. He wasn't as good as Aparicio and those guys. He wasn't Marty Marion, Johnny Pesky, Phil Rizzuto, or Luke Appling, but he had good range and good speed. He could fly to first base. And he had a rifle arm.

The Browns later put Don Gutteridge in to room with Vern. Gutteridge was a teetotaler. I kidded Don. I said, "You didn't stop him from drinking, but he got you to drink." That wasn't true. I don't think Gutteridge ever took a drink.

They said that Vern would die young, and he did, at age forty-four. But he was a wonderful guy.

You know who else could hit? Jack Kramer. In that ninth game that we won in Chicago, Kramer hit a damn ball over the 402-foot sign in left center field.

Jack was a strange guy. He was a fine guy, a handsome guy. He and I roomed together in the Melbourne Hotel in St. Louis, on the corner of Brand and Olive, and we kept it all year. He'd call his mother every night in New Orleans. He had been married to Dotty Dotson, a singer in Del Cordon's band. That Dottie Dotson was beautiful, and she would visit him. She'd come to St. Louis or meet us in Detroit. They finally split. He might have been married twice. Seemed like he was. Jack worked for a milk company down in New Orleans. He was a great advertiser for milk.

"I sell the greatest food in the world, milk," he'd say.

And Jack loved his clothes. He changed his clothes two or three times a day.

They got on him all the time. But if you messed with him, he'd knock you on your ass. I'd say, "You'll find out if you fool with him." You would think Jack was a fruitcake, but he was just the opposite.

Another fine, fine guy was outfielder Mike Kreevich. I love Mike Kreevich. We were about the same size, though he was heavier than me, and he would wrestle me. If he wanted to wrestle you, you had to wrestle back or he'd kill you. We wrestled up and down Pullman cars. The carpet on a Pullman is like sandpaper, very rough, and he'd come looking for me, and he'd be about half loaded. Or we'd wrestle in the hotel.

One night in Washington in the Shoreham Hotel, he found where I was, and we started wrestling, and the whole club laughed all night. Kreevich was the most underrated ballplayer I ever saw, and I've had fifty-nine years in the game. He could hit, and he could run and steal bases, and he could hit with power.

His wife had to watch him like a hawk. In St. Louis, she had him staked out with a one-foot rope so he couldn't drink. But on the road—that's when he drank and when we wrestled. I used to dread him. But he was a hell of a guy. He never got mad. And the index finger of his left hand was cut off.

We played the last seventeen games of the '44 season at home in St. Louis. The Tigers and the Yankees were fighting it out with us. In one game against Philadelphia, we were losing 2–0 in the ninth when a ball was hit into left center and [A's outfielder] Bobby Estalella couldn't catch it. He should have caught it. I had played with Bobby in Cuba, Charlotte, and in Washington. He was a white Cuban, a good guy. He should have caught that ball. Years later, I met Jesse Flores in a motel in Orlando. He was scouting for Minnesota. I hadn't seen him since that game. He said to me, "Estalella should have caught that ball."

We were tied with the Tigers with five games to go. The next day, the Tigers' Hal Newhouser shut out the A's. It was raining in St. Louis. Bill De-Witt had to decide whether to play. He plays the game, and we get beat. Then we played Detroit in a downpour—it wasn't just raining. It was a storm—and Hank Greenberg hit the damn ball out of the ballpark with the bases loaded to win it for the Tigers.

The last four games were against the Yankees. We had to sweep them, and that ain't easy to do. And we did. The game on Thursday was rained out, and on Friday we had to play a doubleheader. There were 700 fans there. In the first game Kramer won when McQuinn hit a home run. In the second game, Nelson Potter won by 1–0. Potter was a hell of a pitcher. Johnny Lindell hit a line drive in that game, and Mike Kreevich caught it behind his head. Ain't nobody but him would have caught that ball.

On Saturday, Newhouse won his 29th game for the Tigers against Washington, but Galehouse shut out the Yankees 2–0.

For the final game, all I know is what I heard. Dutch Leonard started for Washington against the Tigers, and someone offered Leonard money to lose the game. And Dutch Leonard wouldn't have done that for a million dollars. And he beat them with that knuckleball.

It boiled down to one game. We had had a coin flip to see where the game would be played in case of a tie. We lost the toss, and so we would have had to go to Detroit to play it off on Monday. As a result, we all had to pack our bags before that game and carry them to the ballpark. We had to win that final game to go to the World Series.

The night before the game, we met at the Mormon Hotel. Luke Sewell was talking with Zack Taylor, the pitching coach, and one of them asked, "Are we going to pitch one of [the Big Four] out of turn or should we pitch Jakucki?" Jakucki was rested. The others weren't.

Somebody, Luke or Zack, I don't know which one, said, "We'll pitch Jakucki, God dammit. If they start hitting him, we can always take him out. But start him."

In that last game, we got behind Mel Queen of the Yankees. They had us 2–0, and then Chet Laabs hit that scoreboard and tied it 2–2, and the next time he came up he did it again, and then in the bottom of the eighth Vern Stephens hit one over the right field fence over Grand Avenue to beat them 5–2.

There were two outs in the ninth, and Oscar Grimes was the last batter for the Yankees. He hit a foul ball that McQuinn caught, and then George fell into our dugout.

All hell broke loose. There's a picture that went into all the magazines, and I'm in it. I'm between Jakucki; Don Barnes, the owner; and Vern Stephens. Everyone in that picture is gone.

We played the Cardinals in the World Series. They were supposed to kill us, you know. You know who was on that Cardinal team? Mort Cooper, Walker Cooper, Whitey Kurowski, Marty Marion, Johnny Hopp, Stan Musial, and Danny Litwhiler. What a team!

Sewell started Denny Galehouse the first game. We were kinda surprised. We had a saying, "If you get Nelson Potter two runs in the first inning, we can get up and go home." He'll win. A million pitchers can pitch when they're behind. Damn few can pitch when they're ahead. Anyway, get Potter two in the first inning, and we can go home. And Kramer was a hell of a pitcher, and you had Moncrief. Why did he pick Galehouse? But he did. And Denny hog-tied 'em.

Mort Cooper pitched for the Cardinals. Mort Cooper was a load. We only got two hits. Gene Moore hit a single and McQuinn hit a home run over the roof in right field, and we won 2–1.

We have always figured that we should have won the thing. In the second game, we had them 2–1, and Potter picked up that bunt and threw it out into Grand Avenue. That was the turning point in the whole series. We'd have had them 3–1. But for that one bunt. And then that damn guy forced our runner at third base.

He turned and threw in the same motion and nailed him coming into third. And then came the thrown-away bunt. We lost 3–2 in 11 innings.

We won Game 3 by 6–2 behind Jack Kramer. There has never been a better competitor. The son of a bitch would battle ya. He threw them damn screwballs or spitballs. You ain't gonna get eight hits in a row off a screwball. He was one of the first ones throwing it back then.

The Cardinals won the last three games [5–1, 2–0, 3–1]. With our pitching, we were a pretty good match for them. They didn't get batting practice off our guys. I tell you, it would have been great for baseball and for the city of St. Louis if we had won the thing. If we had won, maybe the Browns wouldn't have moved to Baltimore.

We would have won the pennant again in '45 if it wasn't for Pete Gray. He broke up the damn club. We would have won it again. Pete caused a lot of damn turmoil. Mike Kreevich could play a pretty good center field. In the outfield, we had Al Zarilla, Gene Moore, and Mike and Chet Laabs. But when Pete Gray played, somebody had to sit, and goddamn you had to put him out there to let the people see him. So Sewell was between a rock and a hard place. We'd have won it again if it hadn't been for that.

[Note: Pete Gray had one arm and became a gate attraction in St. Louis. He lost the arm as a boy in a farming accident. Gray played one year in the majors with the Browns in 1945, and in 77 games he had 51 hits, six doubles, two triples, while hitting .218.]

Pete Gray. National Baseball Hall of Fame

Pete was an ornery bastard. If you felt sorry for him, he could detect it and he resented it. He was a hard-headed bastard who didn't want nobody feeling sorry for him. He'd get on the train, and when the wheels would start rolling, he'd fall asleep. He would dress up all the time, wore a bow tie and a suit. He wore two-toned shoes, which were very popular back then. The other players would watch him like a hawk waiting for him to fall asleep, and they'd hotfoot him, and everybody would die laughing. He'd stomp his feet like he was putting out a forest fire. His shoes would be smoking.

Pete Gray had about four agitators. Sig Jakucki, Tex Shirley, and Nelson Potter picked on him in a good-natured way. One time, we left St. Louis on the train going on a road trip starting in Cleveland. The day before the first game was an off day, and Luke Sewell went home to be with his family in Akron. He was going to meet us at the ballpark the next day. Whenever the manager leaves, the shit hits the fan every time.

We got on that train, and everybody flocked to the club car, and they started drinking that beer.

Jakucki and Shirley got into it with Pete Gray, and they were half drunk and were about to get into a half free-for-all, when Babe Martin, who could pick up a boxcar, got involved and stopped it. It was a mess. It was terrible. There were other people in the car beside the players. Fred Hofmann and Zack Taylor, the coaches, told Sewell.

The next day Luke called a meeting. Luke took off his coat and rolled up his sleeves, and he was ready to fight. Jakucki was the head honcho in the fight on the train. He started it, and if it hadn't been for Babe Martin, someone might have gotten hurt.

Boy, Luke was furious.

"This is a goddamn disgrace," he said, "to put on an exhibition like what happened on the train yesterday. It's a disgrace to baseball, to the city of St. Louis, the St. Louis Browns, and everybody connected to baseball." And then he said, "The biggest bush bastard I have ever seen in my life is Jack Jakucki."

Jakucki was sitting on the floor, almost behind Luke, and it looked like he was going to get up and get into him.

And Jakucki burst out laughing.

Nothing came of it, but it was a terrible exhibition, and it all started with picking on Pete Gray. It was fun for them but not much fun for Pete Gray.

The guys would make up shit all the time to get on Pete. They called Pete a killdeer with one wing shot off. They teased him, tortured him.

One time, we stopped in Toledo to play an exhibition game. Toledo was our Triple A team. We were standing on an ol' railroad platform waiting for the train. It was blazing hot in the middle of the summer. Someone had turned over a barrel of fish and spilled the fish all over the place. You could smell them in the next town.

One of them bastards went over and picked up one of them small fish, and another one got Pete around the neck, tussling with him, and the first one slipped the fish into his left coat pocket. Pete carried his cigarettes and matches in his left coat pocket.

When Pete put his hand in there to get himself a cigarette, he came up with that dead fish. And Pete just knew that Jakucki had done it. Jakucki was standing grinning and laughing at him, and Pete ran at him and tried to hit him in the face. He hit him in the chest instead. Jakucki was a bull, and they had a little scuffle.

You could write a book about what they did to that guy. Every night, Sig and Tex would get in a barroom brawl.

With about a month left to the season, we were down at the train station fixing to go somewhere, and Jakucki was drunk. He arrived there way ahead of Luke. He had a fifth in his right hip pocket. The liquor is sloshing around. He's gassed up, and he's telling Hofmann and Taylor that he is going to whip Luke.

"I'm going to beat up Luke Sewell when he gets here," he said.

The train was fixing to leave. Hofmann and Taylor said to him, "Jack, get the hell out of here. Don't let Luke see you." Because Jack was already on the fringe of getting kicked off the team for all the shit he pulled.

"Don't let him see you. Get on the train. Get in there." Hofmann said. "Or go home."

"No, hell," said Jukucki. "I am going to whip his ass."

Luke had to get on the train, go to his compartment, and lock the door. Because Jakucki was going to kill him. What Luke was doing was withholding part of Jack's check every month so he'd have enough money to go home. Jack would spend every nickel he made on payday. Anyway, Luke was holding his money for Jacucki's own good so he could get back to Texas. That's what he was so pissed off about.

Charlie DeWitt called the police. The station after St. Louis is Del Mar, and Charlie told the cops, "The train is stopping. Get Jakucki off the train."

When the train arrived at Del Mar, the cops were already there. They went on the train, grabbed him, and took him off.

Sig came to Chicago the next day. They think he rode the freight up there.

"That's it," said Luke. "You're gone."

This was a month before the season was over. That was the first of September, payday.

We still had a chance to win the pennant in '45. Detroit won it when Greenberg hit the home run with the bases loaded in the ninth inning in St. Louis. It was pouring down rain, and he hit that thing off Nelson Potter plum over the hot-dog stand in left field. We should have been playing the Cardinals again for the damn thing. See, Pete Gray, just his presence, screwed up the whole deal.

The owner figured that because he had one arm, people would come to the park. Well, it worked, but we didn't win because of it.

That year, Bobo Newsom was pitching for the A's. Bobo was a fanatic about any trash being on the mound. He'd pick up rocks, anything that was out there, and clean up. Bobo was a landscape man.

We knew that, so Al Zarilla and Mule Byrnes got a piece of paper and tore it into a million pieces. Every time they came in from the outfield, they'd cross the mound coming into the dugout and drop shit on the mound. And Bobo would have to come out there and clean it up.

So now we have Pete Gray leading off, and we're hoping he can get a hit off Bobo Newsom. Anyway, we prayed he'd get a hit to lead off the game, and he did. He hit a line drive to centerfield, and we were all in the dugout hollering at Bobo.

We yelled at him, "Bobo, you are just right for a one-armed man."

And Bobo blew his stack. He walked over in front of our dugout and cussed everybody out.

I'm so glad I got over there with them bastards. Nobody else had a collection of goofs like we had.

• *14* •

Roy Campanella

"I've got some special news for you," Walt said. "After the game, Mr. Rickey wants you to fly to Brooklyn."

"He wants me to fly to Brooklyn?" I said.

—Roy Campanella

$\mathcal{R}$oy Campanella was one of the greatest catchers in the history of the game. A product of the Negro Leagues, he had played for the Baltimore Elite Giants since he was fifteen years old. In 1946, he was approached by the Brooklyn Dodgers to become the second African American to break the color barrier in baseball. After breaking the color barrier in the minors for two years, Campanella became the Brooklyn catcher in 1948 and starred for the Dodgers, winning the Most Valuable Player Award in 1951, 1953, and 1955. He was going to move with the Dodgers to Los Angeles to start the 1958 season when, driving from his liquor store in Harlem late

Roy Campanella. Author collection

at night, his car skidded off the road and crashed into a utility pole. The car turned upside down, as did his life. Campanella suffered a broken neck and spent the rest of his life in a wheelchair. I interviewed him in 1981 for my

151

book *Bums*. Campy died in June 1993. Despite his disability, Campy was one of the sweetest, kindest men I have ever had the pleasure of meeting.

Roy Campanella: When I was in high school in Philadelphia, I purchased my first car for twenty-five dollars. I had to push it off the lot. It didn't run. It was an A Model Ford, the first car with a gear shift and a rumble seat. I bought it from money I had saved up—my mother had saved it for me for my working with the milkman for twenty-five cents every morning. I saved up my quarters and paid twenty-five dollars for the car.

That was one of my first jobs. I was eleven, twelve, and thirteen years old. I approached him one day, and I just asked, "Do you need someone to help you in the morning?"

"Yeah," he said, "I'd like you to help me, but I can't give you more than a quarter a day."

"That's all right," I told him. Because in those days when I was in junior high school, the lunch only cost eleven cents, so it would pay my lunch every day, and I didn't have to ask my parents. Plus, I could save the rest.

And being the youngest of four children, gee, I felt good that I had a job and I was working.

I was only fifteen when I joined the Baltimore Elite Giants in 1937. I was playing in school, and someone had told them about me, and they asked my parents, and my parents said, "We'll let him play, but he can't play on Sunday." Mother never wanted me to play baseball on Sunday. I always went to our Baptist church on Sunday.

You couldn't play on Sunday in Philadelphia, not even the big league teams. The Athletics and Phillies had to play someplace else on Sundays.

Biz Mackey, who was well into his forties, was the manager of the Elite Giants, and he was the first-string catcher. He was a tremendous receiver, very knowledgeable, a switch-hitter, and he played every day. I was only fifteen years old. And I could only play on the weekend.

I felt lost. I had no idea in the world this would be my profession. Truthfully, I wanted to be an architect. This was what I was striving for in school.

The Baltimore Elite Giants had one of the best pitching staffs in baseball, with Bill Byrd, Andrew Porter, Bob Griffin, and Thomas Glover. These four starters could have pitched in the big leagues.

After school let out for the summer, I was allowed to travel with the team. We always traveled by bus. Every team had a bus. My goodness, we played all over the country. The way the booking agents set it up we would make it from town to town. We played under the lights. They had portable lights on stepladders. The generator was in the outfield with wires running all around, and the generator would light the lights.

That was the real start of night baseball. We played on any sandlot field.

Biz Mackey was a top catcher in the league, the best receiver in black baseball, and thank God, at the age of fifteen, I came up under this man. He insisted I sit beside him every day on the bench, and he would talk strategy to me, talk to me about catching, and he insisted I watch him warm up the pitchers going into the game when I wasn't in the bullpen.

I started off on the right foot. This is the greatest asset any young individual can have. In fact, Mr. Mackey was one of the main reasons my father and mother let me go play baseball on the weekends, when I hadn't been able to play baseball on Sunday.

As a fifteen-year-old, I had so many thrills. I'll never forget the day Biz Mackey got hurt, and then Nish Williams, the second-string catcher, got hurt in the same game with foul tips, and then Mackey told me to go in and catch. And that night, Bill Byrd, a spitball pitcher, was pitching. You could throw the spitball in the Negro Leagues.

I'll never forget it. This fella would chew slippery elm and chewing tobacco, and he had the best control of any spitball pitcher I ever saw. And you just did not hit him. He also had a good curveball and fastball, and wonderful control. And he was a good hitter, a switch-hitter.

Biz Mackay advised me, "Warm him up before you catch him so you know how his ball breaks."

I always did that, even in the big leagues. Even in spring training. I caught every young pitcher who would pitch in an exhibition game to learn how he threw the ball and the way the ball would break. And this helped me quite a bit. And it gave the young pitchers confidence that the main catcher was catching them.

I played in the Negro League from 1937 on the weekends until 1946. I even played high school ball, and that's when the owners of the Elite Giants went to my mother and father and asked, "Can Roy quit school and play with us regular? We'll offer you X dollars." And back in those days that money really meant something. My parents agreed because the money helped at home so much. They figured I could always go back and finish school.

The Elite Giants must have given me a pretty good bonus. I don't know how much it was. I never got it. My parents did. But that didn't bother me a bit. And I never did see a paycheck. They sent it to my parents. I just got meal money.

At the end of the season, we would play all-star games against major leaguers. This is how you would find out how to compare yourself to major league players. We'd say, "Gee, these fellows can't do any different from what we can do."

And then in 1945, I went to the Mexican League and played. Quite a few of the big league players were in that league, too—Max Lanier, Sal Maglie, Lou Klein, Danny Gardella. I played with Monterrey. I was the only American on the team, and we won the pennant.

Then, I went to Puerto Rico to play in the wintertime. Luis Olmo was a teammate. He had left the Dodgers and played in the Mexican League with me.

"Why would you leave the big leagues to come to a league like this?" I asked him.

"I wanted to," was all he said.

I never would have done that. It didn't make any sense.

One player I was close to was Josh Gibson. When I began playing, he would call me "little boy." But year after year I grew up. One year playing in Puerto Rico, I led the league in home runs, and this is when Josh said to me, "You're growing up to be a man now."

Josh died young, and I really can't say why. It's one of those things. Nobody can name the day when you're going to pass. Just look, I've been in this wheelchair for twenty-three years. And gee, I was counted out right after I broke my neck, but thank God, I'm still here, and I feel fine. I like to be in the public. I don't miss a game at Dodger Stadium.

Peter O'Malley has given me a job in community relations, and it makes me feel so much better that no medication in the world can make me feel better than the job he has given me.

And this is why I do a lot of work for the President's Committee of Hire the Handicapped. It means so much to a handicapped person to have a job and to have some place to go every day.

After the 1945 season was over, in October I was playing an exhibition game at Newark on a Friday night with a Negro League all-star team. It was the first time I had ever played with Jackie Robinson.

Charlie Dressen was the manager of the Major League all-stars, and during the game I was going out to catch, and he was going to third base to coach. He stopped and said, "Campy, can I talk to you after the game?"

"Sure," I said.

"Can I meet you outside of your clubhouse?"

I said, "All right."

He said, "I wish you would come to the Dodger office tomorrow morning at ten o'clock in Brooklyn."

I went to the Dodger office, and I had a meeting with Mr. Branch Rickey. He had a scouting report on me as thick as three or four inches. And he read it all off to me, and I was flabbergasted. The Dodgers had followed me, and they knew everything about me and my family. My parents, my schooling, everything.

Mr. Rickey asked me what was I going to do this winter.

"I'm going to Venezuela to play winter ball," I told him.

"Do you have a contract with Baltimore?" he wanted to know.

"No," I said, "just a gentleman's agreement. I play with them, and they give me so much a month for playing."

In those days, a man's word was his bond, his contract, and that's all. If you couldn't go by a man's word, it didn't mean too much.

"Don't sign a contract until I talk to you again," he said.

I suspected Rickey wanted me for the Dodger organization, but I didn't sign right then, and I gave him my word. He wanted to know my address in Caracas, Venezuela, because he had future plans for me. The thing was, I was rooming with Jackie Robinson at the hotel, and Jackie told me he had signed with Montreal the night before. It hadn't been released to the press. I told Jackie I had been over at the Dodger office on Saturday, that I didn't sign a contract, but I agreed that I wouldn't sign with anyone else.

Mr. Rickey asked me to keep it to myself, and I did, though I did talk with Jackie about it. When we went to Venezuela, Jackie and I roomed together and we discussed it quite a bit. Jackie was such a tremendous athlete. It was an honor to room with him and play with him. The man could improve by the day, and he would accept any challenge—he had quite a few of them, and he overcame each and every one of them.

After I returned from Venezuela, Mr. Rickey said to me, "Look, I prefer not to send you to spring training in Florida with Montreal, because Jackie is having problems down there. You've been playing all winter. You stay home, and I will see what team we can send you to."

Mr. Rickey also told Don [Newcombe] he couldn't go to Daytona Beach. Because of the [race] problem, the Dodgers couldn't find a team to send us to.

Jackie went to Montreal, and Don and I went to Nashua, New Hampshire. There was a reason we had to go to Nashua. [Rickey wanted them to play up north, where the racism was less, and they were assigned to Nashua, in rural New Hampshire, even though it was only in a Double A league.]

When the Nashua team passed through New York, Mr. Rickey asked their general manager, Buzzie Bavasi, and their manager, Walter Alston, if they would accept Don and me on their team, and both of them agreed. So this is where we ended up, the Nashua Dodgers. And we won the championship of the old New England League in 1946 and just continued on.

People ask me if it was upsetting that there were teams that wouldn't take me. Well, no, it wasn't upsetting because as a youngster I never had this to look forward to. No black had ever played in the big leagues. So what was upsetting? I was getting the chance to play in the big leagues.

The [black] youngster today can say, "I want to be a big league ball-player." I never could have said that. And it never fazed me or ever worried me that blacks weren't in the big leagues. I would go and watch the Philadelphia Athletics play. Gee, Lefty Grove and Mickey Cochrane, Max Bishop, Jimmie Foxx, Eric McNair, Ernie Shore and Jimmy Dykes, Doc Cramer, and a fellow by the name of George Puccinelli in right field. I got the nickname of Pooch from Puccinelli. But as a kid, I certainly was interested in baseball, but I never thought about playing in the big leagues. Never.

There was no bigotry in Nashua, but going to different towns, you always would find a few who would holler and make smart remarks to you. It made you notice how some people could be. My teammates would come to me and say, "Pay them no mind." My teammates were tremendous.

From Nashua, I went to Montreal and played a whole season there. Jackie had left to go to the Dodgers. Our manager was Clay Hopper. That was 1947, and gee, I won the Most Valuable Player Award. I hit good and caught all the games.

The Dodgers opened the season before we did, and as we passed through New York, I went to see one of their games. I was able to go into the clubhouse, and I saw Jackie. I wished him good luck.

I told him, "I'm sure you can make it."

During spring training of 1948 in Santo Domingo, Mr. Rickey called me into his office at the hotel.

"I want you to do me a favor," he said. "I want to bring you up to the Dodgers for spring training, but I'm not going to let Leo play you. I want to send you out to St. Paul to be the first black to play in the American Association. St. Paul has a farm club that I want to be able to send black players to in the future, and I want you to play there for a while, so we can send other players there."

"I'll definitely do it," I said.

During spring training in 1948, Leo asked Mr. Rickey, "Can Campanella come and take infield practice with us?"

Leo always used to hit infield practice, and for some reason he took an interest in me. He watched me, and he told me how impressed he was with my throwing. Leo wanted to play me, but Rickey didn't let him because, as I said, he wanted to send me to St. Paul.

Walter Alston was my manager there. I was leading the league in just about everything, when Walter got a telegram. We were playing in Toledo that night. I caught that game, and for the second game Alston put me in right field. After the game, I was dressing in the locker room right beside him.

"I've got some special news for you," Walt said. "After the game Mr. Rickey wants you to fly to Brooklyn."

"He wants me to fly to Brooklyn?" I said.

I couldn't hardly believe it, but I was called up to Brooklyn in July. The team was in seventh place. They weren't playing good ball. I can remember walking into the clubhouse and being greeted by Dick Whitman, who had been our center field in the minor leagues, and he said, "Campanella's here. We're saved."

I didn't appreciate that too much. I didn't say anything. But in our first series after my arrival, I got nine hits in my first twelve at bats. Leo Durocher, our manager, told me I was going to be the catcher, and I caught every game. Gil Hodges had been the third-string catcher, and Leo told Gil he was going to play first base. And he told Bruce Edwards, who had been the starting catcher, that he was going to play third base. We had had three catchers in the lineup, and that's how we finished the season. And we went from seventh place all the way to battle the Boston Braves for first place. That was the year they won the pennant. We lost out to them by a half dozen games. But we finished third, one game out of second. All the way from seventh.

It wasn't but a couple weeks later when Leo went over to manage the Giants. After that, whenever we played the Giants, it was like the last game of your career you were going to play. It was more like a World Series. I don't care if we were both down in the standings, it was a packed house, always a big crowd, a lot of noise, and it really got to all the players.

Jackie and Leo didn't get along. In 1948, Jackie came to camp overweight. He and Pete Reiser came in fat, and Leo made Jackie and Pete work off the weight. He had Ray Blades hit them fungoes and make them chase them. He told them they weren't going to play until they got in good shape, and Jackie was resentful of Leo doing that.

This didn't help Leo much with Mr. Rickey. This was defeating Mr. Rickey's plans. This is just my thinking, but this may have been one reason Mr. Rickey let Leo go.

I thought Leo was a tremendous manager. I never had a bad word with Leo because he lived and died with me. And I had to read his mind on every pitch I would give. He had meetings every day to go over what he wanted done, who was pitching, how we were going to pitch hitters, where he wanted the infield to play, where we wanted the outfield to play, and he expected the catcher to know every bit of it.

If there were 30,000 people in the stands, and Leo wanted my attention, he had a certain whistle, and I knew it was Leo, and I would look at him, and he would give me a sign right there what he wanted me to do. That's the God's honest truth. He would whistle, and I knew it was Leo.

I loved playing for Leo. Leo was strictly a catcher's man. Everything I did I did through Leo. When I was catching and he didn't tell me what to do, I

Roy Campanella. National Baseball Hall of Fame

had to read his mind. Every day, he would have a meeting with his catcher. Charlie Dressen also did this, and Walter Alston, too. These three strictly managed with their catcher. Leo was so close to his catchers. So was Mr. Rickey because he had been a catcher. Mr. Rickey would sit behind his desk and talk to me before a ball game. One of the main things he told me: "You have to get the pitching staff to respect your judgment and accept the signs you give to the white pitchers."

And I accomplished that.

When I came to Brooklyn, he also told me, "You have to be sincere, know what you're talking about, and give your pitchers ideas, no matter how old they are. Even though you haven't played in the big leagues, you have to be a take-charge catcher." And this has always stayed in my mind.

I can remember one of the first pitchers I caught was Hugh Casey, a relief pitcher who came in in the late innings. [Casey was a racist southerner.] I had never caught him before, and I didn't know he threw spitballs, but that's what he threw me. But I had caught Bill Byrd in the Negro Leagues, so it didn't fool me one bit.

The way I saw it, Casey was trying to help himself get the other team out. But I was able to catch him. I just knew what it was. He didn't want to tell me, but I could catch the ball.

Thank God I got respect from the entire pitching staff. With Montreal, we had played the Dodgers a lot of games during spring training, and they had seen me play against them a lot. Montreal had a pretty good team, all the top minor leaguers.

I wasn't with Leo for very long. I was there two weeks, when he went to manage the New York Giants. We were very surprised.

Rickey got rid of the southern players on the Dodgers who were giving Jackie a hard time. He made a wholesale trade. He sent Kirby Higbe and Dixie Walker and a few other players to Pittsburgh for Billy Cox and Preacher Roe. Preacher was never a winning pitcher with Pittsburgh, but when he came to the Dodgers, he was a good one.

I would say that 1948 season was the start of the Dodger superiority in the National League. We brought up young players like Duke Snider. We brought up Carl Furillo. Gil Hodges, the third-string catcher, came from Newport News. Jackie came from the farm system. Campanella came from the farm system. Carl Erskine came from Fort Worth. In fact, just about everybody who played for the Dodgers came from our farm system.

Jackie was on his toes for everything that would happen. The Dodgers stayed at the Chase Hotel in St. Louis. It was segregated, but the management of the Chase Hotel sent word to our secretary that the black players could stay at the hotel if they stayed in their room. They were not allowed to eat in the dining room, stand in the lobby, or swim in the pool. The black players, Robinson, Newcombe, and me, had a meeting, and we said, "Whatever the majority votes, we'll go with that."

"Personally, I don't like this," I said. If I can stay in the hotel and can't eat with my teammates or walk around the hotel, I'd rather not stay there. And

Newcombe felt the same way. Jackie didn't feel that way. Not that we fell out about it. We just wouldn't stay at the hotel. Jackie stayed, and Newcombe and I went back to a black hotel. The following year, they told our secretary, "The fellows can eat in the dining room and go any place their teammates go." And that's what we finally did in St. Louis.

We played a game in Atlanta, and we got death threats. It was a little scary. We were in Vero Beach when we received the threats. We were going to play the Atlanta Crackers in the Southern League in a weekend series, Friday, Saturday, and Sunday. Mr. Rickey had advised us, "If you get any threats, please bring them right to me."

They were telegrams. One was from the Wizard of the Ku Klux Klan in Atlanta. That was the headquarters. It said, "If you come to Atlanta, we'll kill you. We will shoot you on the field."

We gave it to Mr. Rickey. We had a meeting with Dr. Martin Luther King. He had contacted Mr. Rickey. Dr. King told him, "Definitely see that Campanella and Robinson come to Atlanta to play this weekend."

We went to Dr. Martin Luther King's home and had dinner with him, and during that trip to Atlanta we just about stayed with him. He told us, "Don't worry about these threats. You carry on just what you're doing at the level you're doing it. That's the greatest thing for our country."

They wouldn't let any blacks sit in the grandstands. They made them all sit on the banks of the outfield. Jackie was playing second base and I was catching.

"You got it made," I said to Jackie. "You could run to center field, and you'd be safe. I got to run all the way from home plate."

I was glad when the series was finally over. Jackie and I both had a wonderful series, and the Dodgers won all three games, as expected. What crowds we had! The black fans flooded the banks in the outfield.

We didn't go out and meet the black fans because some of the white fans were for us, too, and we didn't want to overdo it. If they asked for autographs, we gave them. I don't think we ever carried a chip on our shoulder at any time.

Later on, I got to meet Paul Robeson after one of the games. I thought he was a tremendous singer and a tremendous man. Don Newcombe and I were eating at a restaurant, and Paul was there, and he sent word to ask Don and I to come over to his table. So we sat down with him, and we started a conversation, and it was brought up that he said that American blacks wouldn't fight for our country in a war. We had read about some of his comments in the paper. Some may have thought he went a little too far pushing communism over plain freedom.

Jackie repudiated what Robeson said. Jackie got into politics, where Mr. Rickey from the word go asked us not to. Mr. Rickey said, "Being an athlete, people will try to persuade you from one side or the other, Republicans or Democrats. You have to stay in the middle. You're an athlete. Once you have one side against you, this will make you have people hating you and the other side liking you. Stay out of politics. Exercise your vote but don't stand on the corner on a box and say what so and so is going to do for this party or the other."

I took his advice, but Jackie went along with Governor Nelson Rockefeller. I never saw fit to go along with that. But Governor Rockefeller and Jackie were very close. Jackie was a Republican and I was a Democrat. I always voted for the person who I thought was best for our country, regardless of party.

Let me talk about a few of the games Don Newcombe pitched. On September 5, 1950, we were playing a twi-night doubleheader against the Phillies. When we arrived in our clubhouse, someone cut out and put up on the bulletin board a story from the local paper. In it, Mike Goliat, the Phillies second baseman, said, "If all the pitchers were like Don Newcombe, I would lead the league in hitting."

Newcombe pitched the first game that night against Robin Roberts, and Goliat didn't come close to getting a hit. In a nine-inning game, Don only made eighty or so pitches, and after the game Newk got together with Burt Shotton, our manager, and he said, "I'll pitch the second game, too."

And we ended up winning it. Dan Bankhead got credit for the win. I'll never forget that because that was the only time I ever got a broken finger in a game. Puddin' Head Jones, Willie Jones, hit a foul tip, and it hit me on the thumb. It's why my thumb is so puffy. The bone came right out of it.

Believe it or not, I only missed ten games. I was back to catching the eleventh game. They operated on it that night. I was very fortunate. I never did get hurt very much, and when I did, I had good healing power.

In 1950, we lost the pennant to the Phillies on the last day when Dick Sisler hit a home run off Newk to win it for the Phils in the 10th inning. Sisler was a good hitter if you threw him a pitch away. Keep the ball in, and he didn't hurt you. Newcombe had good control, but just let the ball get away from him.

We didn't get too many runs for Newk, and another thing: the pitcher from the other team who faced him was always their top pitcher. When you have to face the best every game, and then if your team isn't hitting, it's a little tough. You have to score runs to win.

In 1951, Newk pitched the final playoff game against the New York Giants. He was taken out in the ninth inning with the lead. I wasn't in the game. Rube Walker was catching because I had a charley horse. I pulled it in Philadelphia the last game of the season. I hit a ball to the top of the right center field fence opening the inning, and with nobody out. I said to myself,

I will try to get a triple. And I wound up with a triple, but as I was running past shortstop, I pulled my right thigh. I dragged my leg into third. That was the day Jackie Robinson hit a home run in the 14th inning to win the game. Then we had the three-game playoff against the Giants.

I played in the first playoff game in Ebbets Field. They gave me some Novocain in my thigh. After the game our manager, Charlie Dressen, told me, "Look, there's too much room to run in the Polo Grounds. I'm not going to let you catch."

I told him, "Don't worry about it. Let me catch."

He said no. Rube Walker caught that day, and Clem Labine pitched a 10–0 shutout, and Rube Walker hit two home runs. Rube was a very good hitter and fielder. He just wasn't fast on his feet.

So Rube was catching the third playoff game when Ralph Branca came in to relieve Newk. Over the years, people have said that Charlie Dressen should have had me in the game. There was a movie about my life on CBS, and Red Barber asked Charlie about that game, and Charlie told Red, "The only thing I would have done, I wouldn't have taken out Newcombe, but I would have put Campanella in the game because he would have gotten Newk through."

I was sitting in the dugout when Bobby Thomson hit the home run in the bottom of the ninth off Branca to beat us. Uh. That was a tough walk across the field to center field to the clubhouse in the Polo Grounds, and when we got there, Branca was sitting in his locker crying. Mr. O'Malley walked into the clubhouse and told all of us, "Fellas, you did your best. Don't worry about it. It's just one of those things."

Mr. O'Malley walked over to Branca and patted him on the back. I thought that was tremendous. I thought that was warm. And his door was always open to his office.

In 1952 and 1953, Billy Martin helped beat us in the World Series. In the seventh game in 1952, the bases were loaded and Jackie was up. I was sitting in the dugout watching, and Jackie hit a pop-up over the mound, and I didn't think anybody was going to catch it. It looked like the whole Yankee infield was undecided. Are you going to take it or am I going to take it? Martin was playing back, and he ran in and caught the ball. If it wasn't caught, everybody was running with two outs, and it looked like everybody would have scored. If it had fallen safe, we would have rejoiced, but it didn't.

In '53, he beat us again. Martin was a choke hitter, and the balls he hit were falling in. You can't do too much about that. If you can get Mantle and Berra out, and Martin comes up and hits a bloop that beats you, that's tough, but that's the way the game goes.

I thought Charlie Dressen was a tremendous manager. He was in the pattern of Leo Durocher. He wanted to coach third base, and he was one of the best third base coaches. He could read pitchers' signals and what they would throw by watching their hands. He could relay them to the hitter and tell you exactly what he was going to throw.

We were playing the Giants in Brooklyn, and the Giants were beating us 2–1 in the ninth inning with two outs. Jackie came up and hit a ground ball to Alvin Dark at second, and Alvin Dark booted it. I was the next hitter, and Dressen called me over.

"Now look," he said, "he's going to throw you a curveball on the first pitch. If it's a good strike and you like to hit it, hit it."

And that's exactly what I did. He threw me a curveball for a strike, and I hit it upstairs in the Ebbets Field bleachers and we won the ball game.

As I rounded third base, Dressen said to me, "Didn't I tell you?"

He was something else. He believed in the catcher. As Durocher did.

In 1954, the Dodgers let Charlie go and brought Walter Alston in to manage. I was very glad, because I had played for Walter in Nashua and St. Paul. The first day he arrived, I went to him and told him, "Skip, don't worry about anything. We'll make it."

We finished second that year. We were right up in it. The next year, the Dodgers finally beat the Yankees in the World Series. Johnny Podres pitched a 2–0 shutout in Game 7.

Podres, who came up from Class D, was a super pitcher. He brought with him one of the greatest change of paces a pitcher could throw. He won two games in that series.

The score was nothing–nothing going into the fourth inning. I led off that inning by doubling off Tommy Byrne. Hodges and Furillo were batting behind me, and they got me to third and scored me. We scored another run in the sixth, and Podres kept getting them out. In the seventh with a runner on first, Yogi hit a fly ball down the left field foul line—Alston had just taken out Jim Gilliam, who was playing left field, and he put Sandy Amorós in. He didn't pinch-hit for Gilliam. He put Amorós in because he had a stronger arm—and Amoros, who was left-handed, caught the ball. It would have been tough for a right-hander to reach out and catch the ball.

Amorós then turned around and relayed it to Pee Wee, who relayed it to Hodges at first to catch the runner way off. He had rounded second, and we made a double play out of it, a tremendous play. That was some catch.

In the ninth, the Yankees hit three ground balls, and that was it. The last one was hit to Pee Wee. At Old-Timers' Day, I asked him, "Who hit the last ground ball to you?" I thought it was Bob Cerv. Pee Wee said, "It was Elston Howard."

That year, I won the Most Valuable Player for the third time. [Campy had also won it in 1951 and 1953.] Well, I have always felt playing with the type of teammates I did, it was easy playing with those fellows because you played with so many good ballplayers. They would bring out the best in you.

I'd say everybody on the team could have been the most valuable player. I mean, some of those fellows, gee, they were tremendous. I just felt that they had to pick one of us, and they picked me. But to me, it was strictly a team effort. I really felt that.

In the 1956 World Series, Don Larsen pitched a perfect game against us. I made the second out in the ninth inning. I went up there thinking, *I'm going to hit a ball away from me and hit it to right center.* I hit it that way, but the pitch wasn't far enough out over the plate, and I hit a ground ball to the second baseman. I didn't get good wood on it.

These kind of games are tough, because Duke hit a couple of balls good that went all the way to the stands, but they were foul home runs. Jackie hit a line drive that hit the third baseman and in the air went right to the shortstop, who threw him out. You don't see plays like that. It's what happens in no-hitters and perfect games. Balls are hit good, but right at people.

To be an athlete and to play every day, when you go out there, you go out there to do your best and to give 100 percent, and if you come out on the short end, you know within yourself you have done your best. If you win, that's great. You want to win. That's the name of the game, but if you lose, you know you've done your best. And you have a chance to come back tomorrow and win again.

Jackie wasn't with us in 1957, and we finished third. At the end of the season, it was announced that the Dodgers were moving to Los Angeles.

A couple months before the season was over, Walter O'Malley came into the clubhouse and told us. We were amazed, but you have to understand that, holy gee, Mr. O'Malley wanted to build the first domed stadium in Brooklyn at the corner of Atlantic Avenue and Flatbush Avenue, where there was plenty of parking and all the subways trains were underneath it.

In fact, he had a miniature of the new stadium in his office, and he showed it to me. It had a collapsible dome that you could open on sunny days to let the sunlight in and close it in bad weather.

Captain Praeger, the same architect who designed Dodger Stadium in Los Angeles, designed it, but all of the local politicians, except the president of the borough of Brooklyn, turned it down. Representative Kenneth Hahn, from out here in LA, came east to get the Washington Senators to move to LA, and in the meantime he came by to see Mr. O'Malley, and they made an agreement.

I was commuting out to LA for Mr. O'Malley every two weeks. He had me out in LA selling tickets to games at the Coliseum along with Pee Wee Reese, Gil Hodges, Vince Scully, and Walter Alston. We worked with our traveling secretary Harold Parrott selling tickets to different organizations.

On the day I was hurt, I was driving from my liquor store at 134th Street and 7th Avenue in Harlem to my home in Glen Cove, Long Island. I was in the store late at night because I was supposed to go on a TV show after the boxing matches at Madison Square Garden with Harry Wismer. The show was supposed to go on around ten, but Harry called me and said, "Roy, I'm going to announce tonight that you're going to be on next week, so we'll have a larger audience. Don't come tonight."

I got in my car and took the Triborough Bridge to the Grand Central, and by the time I got to Glen Cove, the roads were icy, and I was going round a curve, and I applied my brakes, the car went into a slide, and I hit a pole. The car turned over and that's when I broke my neck. It was funny. I knew I wasn't going fast. But that's how it happened. And I wasn't five minutes away from my home.

I never think about it. I put that behind me. I learned how to live with my wheelchair. It's twenty-three years, but I appreciate my family, all the doctors, what Mr. O'Malley did to get Dr. Russ, appreciate what Peter O'Malley has done for me to give me a job here with community relations.

This job is the best rehabilitation an individual could have. My wife has raised five children. All of them have finished college. Three have master's degrees. I'm proud of them, my wife, Walter O'Malley, Peter O'Malley, Mr. Rickey, and I'm proud of the way I've carried myself and what I have accomplished out of the wheelchair and in the wheelchair.

• 15 •

Roger Maris

Mentally, it just got pretty strong—the press before and after ball games and everything—continuous questions, continually trying to be on your guard because there were a certain few who were looking for you to make a slip.

—Roger Maris

*W*hen I was researching *Dynasty*, in the winter of 1973, Yankee president Mike Burke wrote and signed a form letter to former Yankees asking them to cooperate with me in my desire to interview them. Prompted by Mike Burke's letter, all of them did except Joe DiMaggio, who resolutely shielded himself from public view, and for a long while Roger Maris. I had sent Burke's letter to Roger asking for an interview, called his Budweiser beer distributorship in Gainesville, Florida, and even showed up at the plant he owned in Gainesville. In the entryway was a simple glass case, and in it were his two Most Valuable Player Awards. Other than the two silver trophies, there was no evidence that Roger Maris in any way was connected to the beer distributorship.

I spoke with Roger's brother, Rudy, who ran the place. His brother told me Roger wasn't there and pretty much let me know that I was wasting my time trying to track down his famous brother.

On my way back home from Gainesville to New Jersey, I stopped outside Atlanta at the Golden Glove, a country and western bar owned by Clete Boyer. The Yankee third baseman on the phone promised he would meet me there at nine a.m. the next day.

I went inside just before nine a.m. Seated at the bar were a gaggle of men drinking beer. I ordered a beer that I nursed until the afternoon and waited.

Noon came, and then three p.m., and then six, and still no Clete. There was nothing I could do but continue to patiently sit there and wait. Mean-

Roger Maris. Photofest

while, customers filed in, and country music suffused the place. I was told to be patient, that Clete was coming. I waited. What choice did I have? This would be my only chance to interview him.

Just before nine p.m., Clete made his entrance, and to my great surprise and delight walking in with him was—Roger Maris. The two were close, and since the next day Clete was flying to Tokyo to play one more season of baseball—for a million dollars—Roger had come to party with him and see him off.

Clete and I shook hands, and he led Roger and me to a table while he went off to conduct business.

Roger and I sat across from each other. The room was dark, and Charley Pride's singing filled the entire bar. I introduced myself and asked Roger how he was.

"I'm fine," he said, and after that we didn't have much to talk about. I was reluctant to ask him if he would sit for an interview because if he said no, it would ruin our evening, and so we sat there uncomfortably staring at each other. I struggled to find something to say when, after a few minutes, Roger said to me, "Why don't we go outside and talk."

"I'd like that," I said. What I didn't tell him was that I was ecstatic.

I sat on the hood of one of the cars in the bar's parking lot, took my portable cassette recorder out of my briefcase, and began by noting that after he hit all those home runs in 1961, his relationship with the Yankees deteriorated. I mentioned how badly some of the reporters had treated him, how the fans had booed him, and how Ralph Houk did him dirty. I asked Roger about his feelings about all the bad things that had happened to him in New York while starring for the Yankees. Remarkably, he told me:

"I actually don't feel that bad about it. It's something that happened. It's something I had no control over. It was in the writers' control. Things could have been handled a lot better with the Yankees. Who knows how it happened or why it happened, but it's stuff that happened behind me, and it hasn't bothered me. It would have been a lot nicer if it had happened the other way around, but it wasn't."

"It's a shame that after this tremendous feat you performed [breaking Babe Ruth's record of 60 home runs in a season] that it seemed they were holding it against you," I said.

"You might call it that. I guess I did something evidently that was sacred, something I wasn't supposed to do."

"Somewhere along the line it had to affect your play," I said.

"There's no question about it. You don't go out there and play 162 ball games and have people on your back continuously day in and day out, and not have it affect your play. It's got to. It took a lot for myself, personally, going out there every day—naturally, you're trying to do your best, but when all of the elements are somewhat against you, I don't feel I got the best out of me."

"I'm going to ask you a personal question, and it is your privilege not to answer it," I said. "Late in the 1961 season there was a game where your hair was falling out. It seemed to other players you were on the verge of cracking up. You went to Ralph that day."

"I got a day off. I needed it."

"How bad was the tension? What happened that day?" I asked.

"I said it before, and I'll say it again. Pressure, as far as playing the ball game, there was *no* pressure. Playing was the easiest part of it. Mentally, it just got pretty strong—the press before and after ball games and everything—continuous questions, continually trying to be on your guard because there were a certain few who were looking for you to make a slip—I'm not trying to knock anybody, but you know sometimes when you're answering one guy's question, someone else butts in with another thing, and another guy comes in on half of what you said, and they misinterpret. Through all the pressures, the continuous questions being fired at you, the pressure was quite strong. Mentally, I needed time off."

"What happened that day?" I asked.

"Nothing. I don't know. I had already hit the 60th. Steve Barber was pitching, a left-hander. I don't ever believe I hit Steve that strongly. I managed to get a few hits off him, but not that strongly. I was having enough pressure mentally that I just felt I needed the day off, and of the remaining ball games that I had left, to me this was the best day to take. This is when I asked Ralph for the day off, and I got the day off."

"In 1963, your home run hitting declined. Was that an injury?" I asked.

"It didn't decline. I only played in 90 games in '63, and I ended up hitting 23 home runs for 90 ball games. That's 72 short of a complete season, so for the amount of ball games I played, I hit a lot of home runs. Through the course of the season, I was having back problems, and when I got home after the season my neighbor, who was my dentist, came over to the house and asked if I would have my teeth checked. He thought I might have an abscess that was giving me the back problem. He checked it, and sure enough, I had the abscessed tooth, and once I had that tooth extracted, I no longer had that problem. But I still had 23 home runs for 90 games."

"What happened to the Yankees after 1964?" I asked.

"That's a good question. What happened to them? I don't know really how I could answer what happened to them. You had some guys leaving. Bobby Richardson left. Tony Kubek had a pinched nerve. Naturally, Mickey and me and some of the guys were getting a little older. It was a conglomeration of many things. I don't think I can single out just one thing.

"In '65, I had a broken hand all year, and really, once I broke my hand, it was all over for me because right today I don't have any gripping strength in my two fingers of my right hand, so in order to swing a bat and have that end slip out of there . . ."

"How did you hurt the hand?" I asked.

"I slid into home plate, jammed my fingers into the umpire's shoes. He was standing a little bit too close to the plate. This was in May. I dislocated

Roger Maris. Photofest

two fingers, and they pulled the fingers back out and put them back in the joint. That was all right. We left New York the following day and went to Washington. The first time I took a swing in Washington something popped in my hand and that was it. That gave me a long vacation.

"We took X-rays in Washington. We took them in Minneapolis. We took them in New York. There was never any mention of a break, and at first I started out going into the field and taking infield and throwing a baseball. The ball club every four or five days they would ask me to take batting practice. I'd try a few swings, and it didn't work, and it got to the point where I couldn't even throw a baseball because I couldn't hold a baseball in my hand. And yet they were continuously asking me to take batting practice."

"Was this to get the fans to come to the ballpark when they saw you batting?" I asked.

"This I don't know. I can't speak for Ralph Houk, who was the general manager, or Johnny Keane, what the reasons were behind it. I can't speak for them. It's just something I've never understood, how I can go from May to the end of the season to find out I have a broken hand. Granted, it wasn't broken and showing through. But I knew it was broken, and press-wise everybody was, 'Well, once again, Roger Maris is just jaking.'"

"I read that one time even Ralph said something like that," I said.

"Well, yeah. The implications were there."

"That couldn't have helped your disposition."

"That doesn't help anybody because I've always said I'm out there because it was the best way I knew to support my family. And the only way I could support my family was to make good money. The only way I could get good money was to go out there and do the job. If I'm sitting on the bench jaking or otherwise, I'm not supporting my family. It's sort of stupid to have someone come up with something like that.

"It takes all kinds. I know when I ran into the wall in the 1963 World Series—I played one game and a couple of innings—I hit the wall with my left arm and injured it to where it was about a month before I could do much with it. Then I read in the paper that after Ralph reviewed the World Series films, he said he now believes something was wrong with me. It's almost as though he was saying prior to that nothing was wrong with me. These are things you don't understand."

"What an SOB," I said.

"I'm not going to say that. Everybody is going to draw their own conclusions because, like I said, I'm not going to knock Mr. Houk. I'm not going to knock anybody. There are just a lot of things I don't and I never will understand."

"Will you ever come back to New York?" I asked him.

"One day, I will come back to New York. When, I don't know. Right now, I just don't have the desire to. This year, many people wrote me letters asking me to come to the Old-Timers' Game in New York, and from what I understand from friends of mine in New York, the ball club put out the word through the announcers that the reason I'm not coming back is because I'm afraid people are going to boo me.

"For many years I've been booed by the best. For maybe twenty minutes during a ball game? It's not my concern. The ball club is trying to push off this stuff, but Old Roger again. 'You know, the poor boy is not going to come out because the poor boy is afraid of boos.'

"That is *not* the case. I have other reasons why I haven't wanted to go up there. The ball club knows what they are."

"Can you tell me one of them?" I asked. "That way people will understand."

"I understand your point, but you have to understand my point. I've never believed in knocking people. I don't want to knock people."

"These people are gone now," I said. "Steinbrenner now owns the team."

"A lot of those people are gone, but still, it's not in my nature to knock people. If I wanted to write a book, I could write a pretty good one. It's just something I don't believe in doing. The thing is, all you do is reopen wounds. Right now, Roger Maris is in Podunk. No one knows he's around. No one's heard of him during the last five years, and it's beautiful. I hate to reopen an old wound. This is basically what it amounts to."

"How is your beer distributorship?" I asked.

"Very good. I have a good time, and we do sell some beer."

"Thank you."

My interview with Roger Maris was one of the last he gave before his death in 1985. He returned to Yankee Stadium on April 14, 1978, twelve years after his last visit. The packed crowd gave him a standing ovation. In the Yankees dugout watching were manager Billy Martin and coach Yogi Berra.

After the event, Maris was asked why he decided to appear after such a long absence.

"George Steinbrenner has been trying to get me back for several years," Maris said, referring to the Yankee owner. "Why did I finally decide to do it? Because I have six kids, from twelve to twenty years old, and they ask questions. They read through the boxes of stuff, all those clippings that say how awful I was as a ballplayer, and I've got to tell them something.

Roger Maris and Mickey Mantle. Columbia Pictures/Photofest © Columbia Pictures

"So I decided to give it a try. But I have mixed emotions about coming back. There comes a time when you decide to try it. We'll see if it was the right thing to do."

Clearly, the hurt from the way Roger had been treated by the press, the fans, and the Yankee brass had never gone away.

· *16* ·

Monte Irvin

Clyde Sukeforth, the scout for the Dodgers, had Campanella and me come over to the Brooklyn office in October of 1945. I signed with the Dodgers, but I told them I had had a tough time during the war.

"I don't have the skills I used to, and I don't have the feel for the game that I used to." I told them I needed a little time to get my act together.

—Monte Irvin

$\mathcal{M}$onte Irvin was born on February 25, 1919, in Halesburg, Alabama. The eighth of thirteen children, he and his family moved to Orange, New Jersey, when he was young. After starring in four sports in high school, he attended Lincoln University on a football scholarship. He quit after he found his time practicing football interfered with his desire to study dentistry. Meanwhile, Monte was recruited to play baseball by the Newark Eagles in the Negro Leagues in 1938. After starring, he moved on to the Mexican League, where he won the Triple Crown.

He spent three long years in the army during World War II, including fighting in the Battle of the Bulge. As Monte will tell you, Branch Rickey wanted to sign Irvin to play in the major leagues even before signing Jackie Robinson, but Irvin had felt so angry at his racist treatment by white superior officers in the army that he told Rickey he wasn't psychologically prepared to take on the abuse that Robinson would absorb. Rickey signed Robinson after Irvin told him he couldn't do it.

After Rickey refused to pay Newark Eagles owner Effa Manley the $5,000 she demanded to acquire Irvin, he let Irvin out of his contract. Irvin

174

Monte Irvin. National Baseball Hall of Fame

then signed with the New York Giants in early July 1948. He and Hank Thompson were the first African Americans to play on the Giants.

Monte led the Giants to a pennant in 1951 and helped them win a World Series in 1954. After two seasons with the Chicago Cubs, he retired in 1957.

In 1968, Irvin was named a public relations specialist for the commissioner's office under Bowie Kuhn. In 1973, he was elected to the Baseball Hall of Fame. His number 20 uniform was retired by the San Francisco Giants in 2010. After living in Ocala, Florida, he moved to a retirement community in Houston, where he died on January 11, 2016, at the age of ninety-six.

Monte Irvin: In 1942, the Negro League owners and the players took a poll, asking which player would be the perfect representative to play in the major leagues. They said I was the one to do it, the perfect representative. I was easy to get along with, and I had some talent.

Then I went into the war, where I was treated very shabbily. I was with a black unit of engineers in England, France, and Belgium. More than anything else, we weren't treated well in the army. They wouldn't let us do this. We couldn't do that. The guys said, *If they weren't going to give us a chance to perform, to reach our potential, why did they induct us into the army?*

We [African American soldiers] had a lot of problems with our own soldiers and sailors. Other guys said, "Maybe we're fighting the wrong enemy."

We trained at Camp Claiborne, in Louisiana. It wasn't a good situation. There was a black tank outfit at Camp Claiborne, and by the time they came off the field and took a shower, the PX had sold out of everything—no beer, no ice cream, no soda, no soft drinks. The men just got fed up. They got in their tanks and tore all the PXs down with their tanks. They had to send over to Mississippi to get an antitank outfit to stop them. Two weeks later, they were shipped over to Africa to fight. They said, "Damn, they should have done this many months ago."

All of our commanding officers were white. In England, we had a southerner who had no business being a company commander, and he made some remarks about no fraternization with whites, said we couldn't do this, couldn't do that. After he spoke, we had a company chaplain who got up and said, "Men, you're members of the United States armed forces. You can do anything anybody else can do. I assure you, this company commander will be gone in two weeks." And he was. He was replaced by a lieutenant, a black company commander. This was 1944 in England, in a little town called Redruth in southern England.

We didn't think we were ever going to get back home. We felt like we were thrown away. We built a few roads, and when the German prisoners started to come in, we guarded the prisoners. We said, "It would have been better if they hadn't inducted us and just let us work in a defense plant." They wouldn't let us do anything. We were just in the way. They were going to send us to the Pacific, but then after the bomb dropped, they sent everybody home.

I got home on September 1, 1945, and in October I started playing right field for the Newark Eagles. I had been a .400 hitter before the war, and I became a .300 hitter after the war. I had lost three prime years. I hadn't played at all. The war had changed me mentally and physically.

We played an all-star team in Brooklyn. Ralph Branca and Virgil Trucks struck out about eighteen of us. Trucks and I visit every year, and we talk about the old days. I won't say "the Good Old Days." The Old Days.

Clyde Sukeforth, the scout for the Dodgers, had Campanella and me come over to the Brooklyn office in October of 1945. I signed with the Dodgers, but I told them I had had a tough time during the war.

"I don't have the skills I used to, and I don't have the feel for the game that I used to." I told them I needed a little time to get my act together.

They said, "Okay, let us know when you're ready, and we'll bring you up."

I didn't feel I was ready until I played in the Cuban Winter League in 1949. I called the Dodgers and told them I was ready. Meantime, the Eagles owner, Effa Manley, said, "Mr. Rickey, you took Don Newcombe from our team. I'm not going to let you take Monte. You're going to have to give me at least $5,000." So rather than get in a lawsuit, the Dodgers released me, and the Giants gave the Eagles $5,000 and picked up my contract. I didn't get a nickel of it. I asked for half, but Mrs. Manley said, "No, I worked so hard to get this done. I'm going to split it between my lawyer and myself." She took the $2,500 and bought a fur stole with it, and when I saw her twenty-five years later, she was still wearing that same fur stole.

On July 8, 1949, Hank Thompson and I reported to the New York Giants. Leo Durocher came over and introduced himself. When everyone got dressed, he had a five-minute meeting.

"I think these two fellows can help us make some money, win a pennant, win the World Series," Leo said. "I'm going to say one thing. I don't care what color you are. If you can play baseball, you can play on this club. That's all I'm going to say about color."

This was two years after Jackie. They had gotten used to seeing an African American on the field. It wasn't a picnic. We heard the names. But we didn't have it as tough as he did.

When Willie Mays came to the Giants in 1951, we had a perfect team. Leo moved Bobby [Thomson] to third base, Mays to center, and I went from first base to left field. Whitey Lockman came in to play first, and our pitching staff was Maglie, Jansen, Koslo, Hearn, and Spencer. They all had a big season along with Alvin Dark and Eddie Stanky.

The Brooklyn Dodgers had an all-star team, and every time we'd go to Ebbets Field to play, we knew it was going to be a dogfight. They had

Leo Durocher. Author collection

Hodges, Robinson, Reese, Cox, Campanella, Snider, Furillo, Pafko, and a great pitching staff with Preacher Roe, Carl Erskine, Don Newcombe, and Irv Palica—right down the line a great team.

In '51, we won our first game, then lost one, and then won eleven games in a row. We were playing the Dodgers in Brooklyn, and we could hear them in the clubhouse. They were banging on the walls that separated the two clubhouses.

Furillo was saying, "Eat your heart out, Leo. You'll never win it this year." Jackie was saying the same thing. "You'll finish in last place, Leo, you SOB."

"If this is not incentive enough to get us started," Durocher said to us, "nothing will."

We went on the road and won sixteen in a row after that. We were rolling. We had a fantastic year.

"Let's don't give up," Durocher was saying toward the end of the season. "Let's see how close we can come. If we don't win, we've tried."

Leo had a fantastic year managing that year. He liked moving a man over, and Willie Mays was just a perfect young man to have on the team. He didn't hit that much when he first started, but he caught everything in the outfield and threw out everybody who ran, so it was a pleasure to come to the park to see what this talented youngster was going to do next.

Willie was nineteen, and it's amazing what a talented young player can do for a team. It gives you a lift. He makes a key catch or gets a key hit to win a ball game, and you look forward to coming to the game. We couldn't get to the park fast enough to see what this diamond in the rough was going to do.

Leo just kept egging him on. If Willie made a great catch or got a key hit, Leo would hang a new suit up in his locker.

I was twelve years older. Leo didn't have to do that for me. I was going to give my best regardless. We just reveled in Willie's success. We were just happy to have him on our team. We were in the pennant race. Bob Thomson was having a good year. Alvin Dark was having a good year. Don Mueller was a magician with the bat, and I was trying to make a contribution as well. [Monte was being modest. He hit .312 with 24 home runs and 124 RBIs in 1951.]

The 1951 season ended in a tie with the Dodgers. We won up in Boston, and the Dodgers won in Philadelphia. We were listening to the Dodger game on the radio on a train coming back from Boston.

The Phillies were leading when Del Ennis came to the plate with the bases loaded. We figured they would probably get a run. All he had to do was hit a sacrifice fly or a slow ground ball. But they popped him up, and then Eddie Waitkus hit a shot over second base, and Robinson somehow caught

Casey Stengel and Leo Durocher, author collection.

the ball, and the game went into extra innings. And in the 14th inning Jackie hit a home run to win the game.

After the game was over Durocher said to us, "Fellas, let's approach this as though it's the first game of the season. Go right after them tomorrow in Brooklyn."

Jim Hearn beat them in the first game at Ebbets Field 3–1. The next day, we moved over to the Polo Grounds, and Clem Labine shut us out 10–0. Clem had a great sinker and a big jug-handled curve. We hit some shots, but Cox, Reese, and other guys played great.

Big Newk pitched the next day for the Dodgers, and we were behind 4–1 going into the bottom of the ninth inning. We had given it all we had to give, and we were hoping something would happen, and sure enough, Dark singled. Mueller singled. I came up to the plate and fouled out, happy that I hadn't hit into a double play.

One of the key hits was Whitey Lockman's double. He doubled down the left field line, and Mueller went on from first to third easily. He really strained his ankle sliding into third base. Leo took him out and put Clint Hartung in to run for him.

The Dodgers changed pitchers. They brought in Ralph Branca to pitch to Bobby Thomson. Branca had been a good reliever. There was no great expectation, even though Bobby had hit three or four home runs off Branca. So Big Newk went out, and Ralph came in, and he threw a high fastball, a pitch Bobby could really hit.

Now after all these years, I say this: Rube Walker was the catcher. In a key situation like that, you want to make sure you throw a curve away or breaking ball down. Rube and Ralph figured they'd get ahead of Bobby and then really pitch him to get him out. They threw Bobby the same pitch figuring he wouldn't be looking for the same pitch, and that's when he whacked it. We were just worrying whether the ball would be high enough to go into the stands. And when it went into the lower stands, we couldn't believe it. I'll tell you, we looked at each other, and all of a sudden we realized that we had won the pennant.

We ran to home plate, jumping up and down, and as Bobby was rounding the bases, we met at home plate, and I'll always remember Stanky ran out and wrestled Durocher to the ground. Durocher was coaching third base, and Leo was trying to get to home plate to congratulate Bobby, and Stanky kept tackling him.

"Leo, we won it. We won it. We won it."

I talked to Big Newk later, and he told me he didn't even see it. He had been in the shower. He said, "The photographers came into the Dodger locker room and started breaking down their cameras, and I asked, 'What the hell are you doing?'"

"The Giants won the pennant."

"You're full of shit," said Newk. "We had a 4–1 lead. How are they going to win the pennant?"

They broke down the cameras and went across the breezeway to the Giants clubhouse, and sure enough, Newk found out that we had won.

Horace Stoneham, our owner, and our pitcher, Sal Magie, didn't see it either. They were walking underneath the stands to get to the clubhouse when Thomson homered.

They had put the champagne away in our clubhouse when the Dodgers had that 4–1 lead on us, so we had to drink lukewarm champagne, which the guys didn't particularly like.

Willie Mays tasted the warm champagne, and he wondered, *What the hell is that?*

"I have never tasted anything like this before," he said. "Bring me a soda."

"I'll take a beer," said the rest of the guys.

We stayed in the clubhouse, had two or three beers, and some of us had a little buzz on. We then got in our cars and drove home.

So you know everything I know about that series, except that many years later, Bobby and I were at a fantasy camp, and I said, "Bob, tell me this. What do you remember about that ninth inning?"

"Monte," he said, "the only thing I remember is when I came to bat Leo Durocher came halfway from the coaching box to home plate, and he said, 'If you ever hit one, hit it now.' And I don't remember rounding the bases. I just don't remember. I was very, very happy, but I don't remember rounding the bases."

"I remember seeing Robinson standing there as you were rounding the bases to make sure you touched each base," I said, "as if the umpire would have had the guts to call you out if you had not."

"Yeah," Bobby said. "Maybe you're right."

We couldn't have done it without Durocher because he kept egging us on. He made a lot of great decisions. Being part of that team was the greatest thing that ever happened to me in baseball.

We showed up at Yankee Stadium the next day at eleven o'clock, and we were still on a high. We went out and beat the Yankees 5–1. Just great moments. I remember them as if they had happened yesterday.

I stole home in that game, the first time it had been done in about thirty years. Al Simmons was the last player who had done it. I stole home four times that year.

I liked to run. I would get an extra big lead, and when the pitcher went into his pumping action, I'd take off. I saw that Allie Reynolds was taking a long time to deliver the ball, and I thought, *I think I can make it. Get a big lead and go ahead.*

I slid under Yogi safely. The umpire called me safe, and Yogi said, "No, no," and I said, "Yeah. Yeah, yeah."

"How do you know you're safe?" Yogi asked me.

"You'll see it on the front page of the *News* and the *Mirror*," I said.

And sure enough, there it was.

A year later, Jackie stole home against the Yankees. Thirty years later, Jackie and I were on the Veterans Committee with Yogi, when Yogi came over to me and said, "Monte, you were safe. Jackie, you were out."

I said, "You're right, Yogi."

I just wish we had had Don Mueller. He was a hot hitter. He, Bob Thomson, and Alvin Dark were really hitting the ball well. And I was making a little contribution, too.

The Yankees won that series 4–2. DiMaggio played his last game, hit his last home run. It was special playing on the same field as DiMaggio. And

Willie Mays really admired DiMaggio also. He was one of Willie's heroes. We faced Raschi, Reynolds, and Lopat, and Lopat gave us more trouble than anyone with that herky-jerky motion.

Mantle hurt himself in the first game. He stepped on a drain in the outfield. Didn't matter. We lost. But going into the World Series was anticlimactic. We had done what we had wanted to do, which was to win the National League pennant and beat the Dodgers.

I was also part of that Giants team that won the pennant in 1954. I was the right fielder. We were more experienced then. We had a good staff. We had Johnny Antonelli and Rubén Gómez, and we had Marv Grissom and Hoyt Wilhelm as our relievers. We were simply a better team than the Indians were, even though they had three twenty-game winners, Bob Lemon, Early Wynn, and Mike Garcia, and Bob Feller was on the team along with Hal Newhouser. We had played them in spring training, and we knew they didn't have much speed and we had a better defense, even though they had the best pitching staff.

Even though they were overwhelming favorites to win, we knew we could beat them. And the highlight was the great catch by Willie Mays.

I was in right field. Don Liddle was our pitcher, so Mays was playing Wertz to left center. The ball was hit on a line to right center, so he had to leave at the crack of the bat to catch the ball.

Okay, so he goes over and makes an over-the-shoulder catch, and then he had the presence of mind to wheel and throw the ball back into the infield to keep Doby from scoring on a sacrifice fly. He did all that.

Most fielders would have been happy enough just to catch the ball, but as soon as he caught it, he wheeled and threw the ball back to Dark—so Doby didn't score.

We tied the ball game up, and that's when Dusty Rhodes hit the home run to win it. Dusty got the key hit in the second game, so we were on a roll.

The last game was our easiest one. I thought they were going to let Bob Feller pitch, but they brought Bob Lemon back on two days' rest. Bob never won a World Series game. Given the chance to win, Lemon had nothing.

We won 7–4. In a crucial situation, Durocher had taken me out and let Dusty hit for me, and Dusty hit a home run.

"Dusty, I'm not mad at you," I said. "Just keep hitting. How can I be mad at you?"

Consequently, Dusty and I became close friends. We're very close today. He lives out in Las Vegas, and I go out every year or so and we have a ball.

My last year of baseball, the Giants traded me to the Cubs. I made a contribution, even though we finished last. I hit .271 with 15 home runs. I got to be teammates with Ernie Banks and Big Bob Rush, and Warren Hacker. We had Turk Lown, Dusty Baker, and Dee Fondy, our first baseman. It was the best team I ever played on that finished last. We had a young pitcher, Don Kaiser, who from the All-Star Game to the end of the '56 season was one of the best pitchers in baseball. He went to spring training the next year, hurt his arm, and went right out of baseball.

I knew I wasn't going to last too much longer. I broke my ankle in 1952 and came back too soon. It affected my back. My back would get stiff. But I enjoyed playing in Chicago. It was all-day ball, and Stan Hack was our manager, and even though we finished last, I was just so happy I could make a little contribution before I quit.

I got out of baseball and went to work as an area representative for the Rheingold beer company. I did that until 1968, when I went into the baseball commissioner's office as a special assistant to Spike Eckert, the commissioner.

Mr. Eckert didn't stay long. He was a quiet person who didn't know much about baseball. Joe Reichart protected and advised him. The owners saw they hadn't picked the right man, and so they fired him and hired Bowie Kuhn.

Bowie served from 1969 until 1984, and it was wonderful working with him. Kuhn was a lawyer, a great baseball fan, very impressive. So, I had sixteen wonderful years in the baseball commissioner's office.

All in all Bowie had some very difficult decisions to make. Marvin Miller had become very strong as the director of the baseball players' association. So we saw a lot of changes. For a long time, the owners had everything going their way, and now it shifted the other way. I just hope somehow they can moderate things so a fan doesn't have to spend a year's salary just to take their family to a ball game. I just hope they work it out so as not to kill the greatest game that has ever been invented.

Joe Cronin was the president of the American League in 1972. That year, there was a ceremony honoring Jackie Robinson. Jackie was dying and everybody knew it. I was in the commissioner's office as a special assistant.

During the ceremony, Jackie gave a great speech.

"Things are wonderful," he said, "but one of these days I'll be so happy when I can see a black coach over at third base or a black manager in the major leagues."

The powers that be were to assemble on the mound as Jackie threw out the first ball. Bowie Kuhn, the commissioner; Chub Feeney, the president of the National League; and Rachel Robinson were there, and they looked around, and they didn't see Joe Cronin, the president of the American League.

"Monte, would you search out Joe and tell him to join us on the field?" Bowie said.

"I'd be happy to."

I looked around the stadium and finally found Joe. He was having a hot dog under the stands. I walked over to him and said, "Joe, the commissioner is looking for you. He wants you to join him on the field."

Joe looked up and said, "I'm not going to be there."

"Any particular reason?" I asked.

"No," he said. "I just won't be there."

I went back to tell the commissioner Cronin wasn't going to be there.

"He won't be here?" asked Kuhn.

"No," I said. "He said he can't make it."

The commissioner looked as surprised as I did when he told me. He just shrugged his shoulders. I figured that Jackie had tried out up in Boston, and Joe wouldn't sign him, and Jackie had said some things about Joe, so Joe didn't want to have any part of that ceremony.

So that's my baseball career, Peter. I retired to Florida in 1984, and I still live in Homosassa, Dazzy Vance's hometown, Mike Hampton's hometown, and I hope to live a few more years to enjoy it.

You know everything I know.

Jim Bouton

The function I performed for *Ball Four* was basically a reporting one. Lenny spent one day with the Seattle Pilots. The book is 90 percent anecdotal, and maybe half of it is in quote marks. So I was the reporter on the book. I was the source. The anecdotes were all mine.

—Jim Bouton

*W*hen Jim Bouton was scheduled to pitch for the Atlanta Braves in 1978, it was almost fifteen years since he had starred with the Yankees. But the guy loved baseball, and after learning a knuckleball, he worked hard enough and was good enough to get a couple of starts in the majors again. Jim sent me a plane ticket to Atlanta to see him pitch.

When I interviewed Jim for *Dynasty* in 1974, it was only four years since the publication of *Ball Four*, his best-selling diary of his years with the Yankees and the expansion Seattle Pilots. The book was a sensation. The authors, Bouton and sportswriter Len Shecter, had pulled back the curtain and entertained baseball fans with what *really* went on behind the scenes. The blowback was terrible. Baseball people like Commissioner Bowie Kuhn, Hank Aaron, and Mickey Mantle came down hard on Bouton for breaking baseball's first commandment: *What you hear and see here, stays here.* Bouton became a pariah.

As we talked about how and why he was able to write *Ball Four*, Jim made it clear that the downside of writing his classic was that Mickey Mantle would no longer speak to him. In fact, Jim said, he no longer could go to Old-Timers' Day because Mickey told the Yankees that if Bouton went to the event, he would stay home. Jim found it hard to admit, but he was heartbroken.

Jim Bouton. CBS/Photofest © CBS

Jim Bouton: *Ball Four* came about in 1968. Len Shecter had just done a story about our adoption of David, and he said, "Why don't you keep a diary of the 1969 season and talk into a tape recorder every night. Maybe there will be a book in it."

I had spent the previous year in the minors, so this was going to be a book about a minor league team. I had a shot at making the Pilots, but I was one of fifty pitchers in spring training.

During my first minor league spring training, I had thought about writing a book myself.

Wouldn't it be great if somebody wrote a book about baseball? I said to myself. *A real book because these other books are such bullshit. Books for kids twelve years old. But baseball is so much fun, so exciting, and there are so many great stories to tell.*

I was assigned to Columbia, South Carolina, and I got off the train late in the day, went to my room around one in the morning. There was a line of guys outside my door. My roommate was at the head of the line. There was some local talent in there entertaining the ball club, one at a time.

Geez, I thought, *if this is what baseball is going to be like, I think I'm going to like this.*

I grew up on Chip Hilton stories. He was the all-American boy. He worked at the soda shop. His mother was a widow, and in basketball, instead of winning the scoring championship, he passes off to another kid so the kid can get a letter. There weren't any like that in baseball, except maybe Bobby Richardson.

Lenny Shecter and I were very close. I liked him, for one thing, because he had tremendous courage. I can remember him doing a tough piece on the Yankees, saying that the players wouldn't talk to reporters, or they were angry that he wrote about Bobby Richardson's religious beliefs and his racism. The clubhouse would be boiling.

Lenny was always more interested in the people than the scores, and he felt the truth was more interesting than the big bullshit the writers felt they had to give you. Lenny was a reporter, and the Yankee players didn't like that.

There was a fight on the team bus one time, and the writers all agreed they wouldn't write it because they thought it would hurt the club's chances. Lenny got off the bus and ran to a telephone and phoned in the story. That's the kind of guy Lenny was.

They were just enraged.

As I said, I liked Lenny because of his courage. The clubhouse would be ready to kill Lenny, and, Jesus Christ, here he comes. It was like Dodge City, with everyone with their guns drawn, and here he comes riding into town with his hands on the reins.

It was incredible. Not many reporters would do that in a very hostile situation. In fact, Mantle once told him, "I'll give you one thing, Shecter. You have a lot of guts."

Lenny was also marvelous company. He lived life with a passion. He got angry passionately, and he really had a good belly laugh, a wry look at the world, and a great wit. Sitting down to dinner with Lenny was never a dull experience. He was just so much fun to be with. Sure he was irascible, but I never saw that as a drawback. I loved his attitude and personality. I thought that made him an interesting guy.

And, of course, once we began working on *Ball Four* together, we really formed a very deep relationship. The project meant so much to both of us. He said to me about the book, "You know, there is no point writing another baseball book. Unless you're going to write something that hasn't been written before, then why add to the English language?"

Lenny always called our book "the definitive work on baseball."

It was really a fifty-fifty project all the way. The only writing experience I had was a couple of creative writing courses in college. I had written a couple magazine articles, so I could put words on a page. I did a story about going back to the minors for *Sport* magazine. I could express myself.

The function I performed for *Ball Four* was basically a reporting one. Lenny spent one day with the Seattle Pilots. The book is 90 percent anecdotal, and maybe half of it is in quote marks. So, I was the reporter on the book. I was the source. The anecdotes were all mine.

Lenny did the first editing job. I kept notes during the daytime, and at night I'd talk my notes into a tape recorder and send the tapes for Lenny to transcribe them. Lenny would go through and rewrite what needed to be rewritten and eliminate what needed to be eliminated. He made carbon copies, so I was also going through it. Lenny was the one who did the polished writing. That's why it flows so nicely.

We did have some arguments. We'd sit down and argue, scream and holler, until we finally agreed. At times, we'd compromise, but that was rare. People say to me, "Shouldn't you have left out that one story about Mickey Mantle on the roof of the Shoreham Hotel with a telescope?" That's funny. Everyone thinks if I had left out just one part of the book, no one would have gotten mad. And everyone has a different part that should have been left out! Someone said, "If you had left out the part about Mickey slamming the window down on the kids trying to get his autograph, you'd have been all right." Another person said, "If you had left out the part about Ray Oyler saying he had to leave me for a great piece of ass," everything would have been all right. "If you had left out the part about Pagliaroni saying, 'Okay, all you guys act horny,' everything would have been all right." It turns out if I had left half the book out, no one would have gotten mad.

Most of the guys feel they have an allegiance to Mickey because he's such a great guy. He *was* such a great guy. He really was. He was terrific to the other ballplayers. He was fantastic. He was always making up jokes. I put this in *Ball Four*. People tend to gloss over it. Incidentally, I wouldn't have thought people would have gotten upset about the story of being on the roof of the Shoreham Hotel. The players said, "That SOB Bouton was up there with us, and he was leading us, and he made it sound as though everyone else was doing it but him."

These guys haven't read it. In the book I say, "Here we are on the roof of the Shoreham Hotel with Mickey Mantle." It wasn't said in a terrible or perverted way, but here I am, half the ball club is up here, and I'm with Mickey Mantle on the roof. I don't believe it! In that vein. Later in the book, when I'm with the Pilots and we come to Washington, I take Pagliaroni up to the roof of the Shoreham Hotel to do exactly as we did before. I didn't consider anything wrong with that. What was it? It was probably an advanced form of peeping tom. Worse crimes have been committed.

Jim Bouton. United Artists/Photofest © United Artists

My feeling is that most of the guys who didn't like the book either feel an emotional allegiance to Mickey or they didn't read the damn book. All they hear is the one-line quote someone throws at them.

"Hey, did you hear in Bouton's book, he said such and such?"

"Oh, he did?"

If it had appeared in context with the flow of the book, offset by all the surrounding material which was sympathetic toward the ballplayer's view, it would have been okay.

Bowie Kuhn called me into his office. He thought I made it up. He thought it was all lies. I'm not kidding. He thought I made the damn book up! I hadn't. We actually did kiss on the bus. One night, we got a little drunk. I couldn't believe guys could act that way. I guess Kuhn had gone to prep school, and he couldn't believe this behavior was going on. Listen, it's not just ballplayers. The worst guys in the world are the Shriners or the Elks or the Moose. When they came to Cleveland for a convention, they wandered downstairs in their underwear and threw beer bottles out the windows, and Christ, we're nothing compared to that! A baseball team is like a small mini-convention traveling around the country. When the Shriners get together, it's once a year. They don't hold anything back at all. Running around the roof of the Shoreham Hotel would be light work for some of those guys.

Did you mention *Ball Four* to Mickey? No? Good thing. Mickey has such a strong feeling against me. In fact, there was a CBS reporter in Dallas who went to do a phone interview with Mickey, and Mickey agreed. Mickey told the guy that he would not come to the Old-Timers' Day Game if I'm going to be there. That's why the Yankees have never invited me back to Old-Timers' Day. The reason I'm not invited is that if I am invited, Mickey won't go.

I've thought about calling Mickey. It's a very awkward situation because I'm sure he has a hatred of me that's beyond all reason. It's an emotional thing. He hasn't read the book. He's heard the very worst that I've said about him, and it was probably told to him in the wrong manner. For instance, the whole feeling of why we were on the roof of the Shoreham Hotel. He has heard that I accused him of some sort of perverted behavior on his own, slinking around at night.

It was absolutely not told that way.

I think I feel worse about that than anything related to the book—more than anybody else's reaction to the book. Because I felt in many ways the same way the other guys do about him. They all loved him. I loved him also.

He was great around the clubhouse, told great stories, and was just fun to be around. He was great with me. When I was a rookie, he was nice to rook-ies. After my first shutout, he laid out white towels from the clubhouse door to my locker. Those are things I will never forget as long as I live. God, there were so many reasons to like the guy. You know what I mean?

He played injured all the time. Christ, Mickey was exciting as hell. My first World Series win was 2–1 over the Cardinals. Mantle hit a home run in the ninth inning off Barney Schultz. I jumped on Mickey's back that day. I told about those things in *Ball Four*, but no one will tell him about them. He'll never read about them. He'll never listen about them. So, he'll never know that, yes, I had those feelings for him, too.

It's just that when I wrote the book, I had a reporter's eye for the game. Do you see what I mean? Rather than a ballplayer's eye, and that's why my book is different from other ballplayers' books. The reporter in me had to report the problems Mickey had with the press, had to report the times he turned down people for autographs. Rudely. Not, "I'm too busy. I can't sign." But, "Beat it," slamming bus windows down on kids.

The reporter's eye in me saw those things. But the ballplayer in me still loved the Mickey that was so much fun to be around and play ball with. On the other hand, the reporter in me couldn't close my eyes to the other things I saw about him.

So now the book is out, and he's been told the worst, and so the reporter in me says, "Listen, you did right, and you did a good job reporting and you were honest." So I did the right thing.

On the other hand, the ballplayer in me is saying, "Jesus, what happened to the relationship that you used to have with Mickey?" One night in a bar, he once told me that I reminded him of Whitey Ford because, he said, I had the same guts that Whitey had. When it came down to the clutch, I would throw my best curve on three and two and a man on. To hear this from Mickey Mantle was a great thing. So, the ballplayer in me feels very, very unhappy about what happened with *Ball Four*. On the other hand, the reporter in me says, "This is how you write a book, and you'll have to live with it."

So, I have those two feelings.

And so, I anxiously inquire about how Mickey feels about *Ball Four*, how he feels about me now. The ballplayer in me wants to know. The ballplayer in me is anxious to hear. The reporter in me really shouldn't care.

I would like to tell Mickey—in fact, I have already told [PR Director] Bob Fishel. When I say I haven't been invited to Old-Timers' Day, it isn't because I want to be. I would not want to be invited to Old-Timers' Day ever again. I would never go anyway. If I was invited, I would immediately write them a letter saying, "I'm not coming." Because of the off chance that Mickey might not come. Even if he said he was coming, I could not be sure. I would still be afraid that at the last minute he would say something or he'd feel uncomfortable and not show up. Or say he got sick. Can you imagine

Bouton family photo: Bobbi, Jim, Michael, David, and Laurie. Pictures by Pitcher (Jean Pitcher), Ridgewood, New Jersey, Fall 1968

them announcing my name and having me run out to the foul line and then not announcing Mickey?

Mickey represents the Yankees. I don't.

I don't think he ought to feel that way about me, but nevertheless he does, so there's nothing I can do about it.

While working for CBS Sports a few years after my interview, Bouton attempted to visit the Yankees clubhouse on Old-Timers' Day for a story but was summarily tossed out by Yankee manager Billy Martin.

Mantle died in 1995. Jim's daughter, Laurie, the light of Bouton's life, died in August 1997 when a dump truck lost its brakes and crushed her car. She was only thirty-one. Jim was devastated. Her death led his son Michael to write the Yankees pleading with them to let his father attend the Old-Timers' Game. Bouton returned in July 1998. Some of the old-timers shunned him.

On 2012, Bouton had two strokes and then suffered from dementia until his death on July 10, 2019. It was his death the prompted me to start this book. I loved the guy. All his friends did.

Index

About the Author

Peter Golenbock has written more than sixty books, including ten *New York Times* best sellers. Among his best-selling books on baseball are *Dynasty: The New York Yankees, 1949–1964*; *The Bronx Zoo* (with Sparky Lyle); *Number 1* (with Billy Martin); *Bums*; *Balls* (with Graig Nettles); *Wrigleyville*; *The Forever Boys*; *Fenway*; *Amazin'*; *Idiot* (with Johnny Damon); and *House of Nails* (with Lenny Dykstra).